LANDSCAPES OF THE DARK

To Rosemary,
with much affection

[signature]

LANDSCAPES
OF THE DARK
History, Trauma, Psychoanalysis

Jonathan Sklar

KARNAC

The use of two extracts of the poetry of Anna Akhmatova, reprinted with permission of the publisher. Cannongate Books: *The Complete Poems of Anna Akhmatova* translated by Judith Hemschemeyer, first published in Great Britain by Canongate Books Ltd, 14 High Street, Edinburgh, EH1 1TE.

Excerpt from *The Theatre and Its Double* by Antonin Artaud, copyright © 1958 by Grove Press, Inc. Used by permission of Grove/Atlantic, Inc.

Paolo Uccello, Saint George and the Dragon. Bought with a special grant and other contributions, 1959 © The National Gallery, London. Reproduced with kind permission.

First published in 2011 by
Karnac Books Ltd
118 Finchley Road
London NW3 5HT

British Library Cataloguing in Publication Data

A C.I.P. for this book is available from the British Library

ISBN-13: 978-1-85575-892-6

Typeset by Vikatan Publishing Solutions (P) Ltd., Chennai, India

Printed in Great Britain

www.karnacbooks.com

For Clea and Livia
and
my mother Joyce

CONTENTS

ACKNOWLEDGEMENTS

I want to thank my analysands for their creative contributions to this work. Also, it is a great pleasure to be book-ended, as it were, between my two dear friends and colleagues, Christopher Bollas, who has generously contributed an Introduction, and Michael Parsons, the co-author of the final paper. "The Life Cycle of the Analyst" was originally given to the British Psychoanalytic Society in 2000, but despite Michael's and my best efforts, it failed to be accepted for publication. I have long felt that it contained a too contentious idea: that analysts, towards the end of their careers, might benefit from being in a group process in order to examine clinical endings, including the ending of their own clinical career. Now this paper has a home.

I want to thank colleagues who have listened to and critiqued various of these writings, including my friends in theothergroup, the 1952 Club, Michael Parsons, Roger Kennedy, and Rosemary Davies in my London Continuing Professional Development group, and in Zurich the group of Peter Wegner, Eva Schmidt-Gloor, and Nicole Carels. Teaching the course on "Ferenczi and Contemporary Psychoanalysis" at the Institute of Psychoanalysis, and the University College London MSc, over several years, as well as the American colleagues I have been working with termly in Chicago have been invaluable experiences to hone my ideas. For many years now, I have worked with members of the International Ferenczi Society, and in particular Judit Szekacs. Working for four years from 2008 as Vice President of the European Psychoanalytic Federation has been invaluable in meeting colleagues and thinking about similarities and differences in psychoanalysis throughout the region. My thanks to all those many colleagues for our discussions on theory, practice, and analytic politics. Ruth McCall was a great sounding board for ideas and early editorship, and my thanks to Sophie Bennett who retyped drafts tirelessly. Oliver Rathbone of Karnac has gently steered me to publication.

Lastly, I want to thank Jacqueline Rose for her knowledge on matters analytic and beyond and for her patience with my writing skills.

Notes on publication

A very early version of Chapter Two was published, in Portuguese, in "Formulation of interpretation in clinical practice", *Revista Brasiliera de Psicanalise, xxv(4)*, 1991.

A version of Chapter Three was published in "Hysteria and mourning: a psychosomatic case", Special Issue on Psychosomatics, *Journal of the American Academy of Psychoanalysis and Dynamic Psychiatry, 36(11)*, spring 2008.

A version of Chapter Four was published in "Regresion en la Psicosis y la Histeria", *Revista de Psicoanalisis de la Asoc. Psic de Madrid, 28*, 1998; and "Regressione nella Psicosi e nell'isteria". In: *La Partecipazione Affectiva dell'analista* (Ed. Borgogno), 1999.

Chapter Six was published in an early version in "Psychosomatics and technique", *American Journal of Psychoanalysis, 67*, 2007.

A brief version of Chapter Eight is to be found on the IPA Electronic Newsletter, 9, May 2010, published in "The lifecycle of the psychoanalysis."

ABOUT THE AUTHOR

Jonathan Sklar, MBBS FRCPsych, is a training analyst and fellow of the British Psychoanalytic Society. Originally trained in psychiatry at Friern and the Royal Free Hospitals, he worked for four years in psychotherapy at the Tavistock Clinic in London. For many years he was consultant psychotherapist and head of the psychotherapy department at Addenbrookes and Fulbourn hospital in Cambridge. He now works in full time analytic practice in London. He teaches and supervises at the Institute of Psychoanalysis; teaches an MSc course on "Ferenczi and Contemporary Psychoanalysis" at University College London; and teaches in Chicago. For the past five years, he has convened a psychoanalytic conference outside Cape Town and, for thirty years, has convened Balint groups working with general practitioners and psychiatrists. He has lectured widely throughout Europe as well as in South America. His psychoanalytic papers have been published in Italian, Spanish, French, and Portuguese. From 2007–2011 he was Vice President of the European Psychoanalytic Federation.

PROLOGUE

In the following chapters, we will meander around many linked
analytical subjects, focused on case histories whose subjects range
from neurotic, hysteric, to psychosomatic and schizophrenic analysands. These clinical histories are interspersed with reflections on the
atmosphere of the clinical setting, the use of interpretation, regression,
dreams, and daydreams in theory and also in technique. Throughout,
I argue for a return in analysis to the unconscious value of clinical history and of free association. For Freud, value resided in the giving of
interpretation, to which Ferenczi added the key parameter of "being
in the experience", a difference that I see at the centre of contemporary
debate in psychoanalysis, and which I examine in these essays through
a focus on trauma and its history in psychoanalysis. In particular, the
evocation of the real that is early trauma and its subsequent mental
development are explored in three analyses: one with a schizophrenic, a
second analysis with a man with a severe tic (spasmodic torticollis), and
the third a neurotic with a somatic resistance to ending a long analysis.
The essays are punctuated with many brief and, at times, shocking clinical vignettes to examine the unconscious process, resistance, and the
value of psychoanalytic listening.

The realization of a traumatic past, often in early life when there has been an environment with too intrusive or too absent a carer, leads to early defensive splitting of the ego, which, together with *après coup*, becomes part of the unconscious development of the individual. Even if the analysand as a child or adolescent had been told some of that history, it is usually accepted with perplexed intellectual understanding, which if anything has made it harder for it to find its place within their conscious character. Even though, as these essays will show, it is crucial not to restrict the concept or origin of trauma to the early relation of mother and child, one can view the infant feeding situation as broadly containing three possibilities, two of which contain the seeds of trauma: the mother who cannot bear to look at her baby—leading to the child growing up with a sense of never really having been seen; the mother with such anxiety and paranoia that she cannot take her gaze off the baby—leading to a sense of suffocation of the child; and thirdly, the "good enough" situation in which the mother looks at the baby and looks away in a to-and-fro (e)motion mirrored by the baby. It is central to my argument that much analytical exploration of early trauma does not occur within the intellectual component of interpretation. Rather, it comes about by being discovered in sometimes intangible fragments which can appear as enactments, enabling the unconscious affect of the child to emerge and to be felt by the analytic pair. It can thus begin to be noticed as an experience within oneself and then understood. Such moments in analysis are far different from being told that this or that happened in the then and the now. I also suggest that the position of the analyst must be seen as the expression of her or his own (analysed) character, and that the desire to belong can drive the analyst to take particular theoretical positions. Finding her or his creative direction is often, if not invariably, a long time coming. It is a paradox of, or at least a tension inherent in, analysis that the analyst must both survive alone and also in the presence of the other. An attempt to convey something of this complexity is at the heart of the essays that follow.

The book ends with a brief examination of trauma within European culture, as exemplified by a nidus of totalitarian scars within European analytic societies. For Edward Said, listening contrapuntally was a way of creatively negotiating and discriminating profoundly divergent ways of understanding. I suggest that such a way of listening, in theory and practice, can be a way forward in combating totalitarian states of mind, both in the traumatized individual and also in society.

INTRODUCTION

Christopher Bollas

"The essays are punctuated with many brief and, at times, shocking clinical vignettes to examine the unconscious processes, resistance, and the value of psychoanalytic listening", writes Dr Jonathan Sklar in the Prologue to this remarkable, indeed unique, book that epitomizes a specific tradition of clinical thought. Freud tolerated Ferenczi's shocking clinical examples and clinical inventions because he surely sensed that either Ferenczi was seeing patients he had not seen before or, more likely, that Ferenczi was seeing what Freud could not allow himself to experience and therefore to see.

What was that?

What Ferenczi saw was the arrival in the transference, and in the emotional experience of the psychoanalyst, of deeply traumatic early experiences that had been experienced in "the Real"—to invoke Lacan—and which could only be recalled in the course of analytical treatment. Although of course Freud more than recognized the significance of the transference neurosis and the value of the re-enacted, he was not temperamentally suited to this form of memory. As the one who heard the suspects of unconscious thought revealed in the unwitting unconscious of the analysand, as the one who then put his findings together in the rather neat—at times, astonishingly complex—interpretations that summed up matters of the mind, Freud rather avoided the "mess" of the affective, the love-dripping, or hate-filled, or need-determined realities of his patients' real lives.

In tolerating Ferenczi, Freud allowed a part of his own personality to go forward through the thought of a colleague whom he knew could follow psychoanalysis in ways that he could not bear.

The history of psychoanalysis can be read in terms of writers who focus on what they can tolerate, leaving it up to colleagues to write up the rest. If Ferenczi worked through for Freud what Freud could not consider in his own mind, then it is not surprising that Ferenczi passed on this delegated task to those whom he taught. One of his student-analysands was Melanie Klein, who was to imagine the first year of life in ways unimaginable to Freud. From this split, an entire school of thought, perhaps a movement, was founded around a lack in Freud, its fulfilment promised in Klein.

Klein's task was risky in some ways, as she would be held to task-for what she imagined an infant to be "thinking", but Ferenczi and his colleagues were left with a more challenging one. What resided in the unconscious from the self's real relations to the mother and father, not the psychic reality of "phantasy" conveyed by the analysand in the course of analysis? Freud's belief, belied by his less than genuine apology for mistaken judgement, that the reality of a patient's life is delivered in the name of narrative and not as a recollection of reality, permitted him to avoid the deeply challenging question of what happens to the mind of an infant, a child—indeed, all of us—when we bear a scar imposed upon us from the real? Not the retractable licence of the phantastical, but the unmoveable thingness of reality.

Ferenczi's tradition of thought moved after his death to differing places in Europe, America, and elsewhere. Those who have thought within his tradition—even as Freudian analysts—have never had an easy time of it. Nor would they have expected as much, whether a Franz Alexander, a Michael Balint, or a Jonathan Sklar. Any analyst speaking up for what he believes his patient has told him from the real-transference (as opposed to the projection of endopsychic possibilities), who has brought the terms of his or her suffering *as is*, presents colleagues with what can seem an insoluble dilemma. As Winnicott stated, it would all be so much simpler if analysts could regard patients' narratives as simply the outcome of phantasy. What could one do were they manifestations of reality?

The *other* side of projective identification is not what the infant projects into the mother, father, or environment, but what has been projected into the self from without. Although Ferenczi, Balint, and those influenced by his tradition of thought never put it precisely that way, that was nonetheless what they were trying to understand as they examined basic faults in the self that were the outcome of early infantile trauma.

Balint was kept on the margins of the British Psychoanalytical Society for quite some time. The Society was caught up in enough conflict as it was between Anna Freud and Melanie Klein.[1]

One must be sympathetic to the demands upon a group in the early 1940s of having to find room for the extraordinary encounter between Anna Freud and Melanie Klein, between polar opposites in the conceptualizing of all the major issues in psychoanalysis. Although Winnicott, as well as like-minded colleagues, were present during some of these debates, they remained either silent or eminently politic. But when the clouds of war—the Second World War and the Freud–Klein—were lifted, the British Society was relatively free to fashion its future.

Until then, there had been little time to allow the marginal "drifters" of psychoanalysis to come to London, not only in the figure of Michael Balint, initially resettled away in Manchester by Jones, but for what he represented. If Winnicott had a courage of written conviction, he was the quintessential insider, the figure who really did wish he could bridge Klein and Freud. His true beliefs and his writings said *otherwise*, but he was never at ease with being an outsider, and even as he fashioned the most original ideas of his time, he was curiously at odds with his own inventiveness. Perhaps he tired of constantly repeating his own mantra, that the infant's actual dependence upon the mother would become a fact in the analysis of many adults. Eventually, perhaps tired of the Kleinian wall that could not hear him, Winnicott became more insistent about his own views—that the infant's early reality of the actual object world was inscribed in the unconscious and transferred itself to all other relations.

The other voice saying this was Michael Balint. But Balint was no politician and hardly interested in courting Klein. Indeed, he was often viewed as too difficult and argumentative, a view held by his wife Enid Balint, who believed Michael was not his own best advocate.[2] Be that as it may, Balint was a straight-talking analysand of Ferenczi who obviously decided to make a name for his views even if cast in the strange lingo of forgettable terms, like "the ochnophil" or "the philobat".

By the time Jonathan Sklar began his training at the Institute of Psychoanalysis, what we know of as the Independent Group was waning. Balint and Winnicott had died within a year of each other in the early 1970s. Their most gifted progeny—John Klauber and Masud Khan—would be unable to carry on the torch. Klauber died in the early 1980s; Khan was gone from mental illness in the mid-1970s. Although Adam Limentani and Pearl King carried on, both were more political thinkers than original writers and always had a look-in to see where they were positioned within the politics of the British Society. Marion Milner's brave and singular literary voice was never matched by her quasi-adolescent personal coyness, shying away from controversy of any kind. Nina Coltart, Harold Stewart, and Eric Rayner, on the other hand, continued to present their work to the Society within the integrity of what had certainly been an "independent tradition".

But at this same time, a now-and-then question "are we the middle group or the independent group?"—surfaced in the discourse of Independent Group meetings.[3] This issue is too complex to explicate here, but it is important to understand that Jonathan Sklar is an Independent Group analyst and not a Middle Group analyst. The distinction is political. Middle Group analysts were for the most part Anna Freudians who sought training in the Institute but could not be in analysis with someone whom they knew, so they sought training with an Independent Group analyst. They remained refugees in the Independent Group to the point of contributing to this being an existential Middle Group.

At the time of Sklar's training, the "gentleman's agreement" had prevailed for more than two decades. This meant that when it came to assigning members to one committee or another, the Society placed a Kleinian, an Independent, or a Freudian in a way that allowed proportional representation.

Unfortunately, in the early 1970s a few Independents went into analysis with Kleinians—not itself unusual—but in violation of the gentleman's agreement, they unfortunately became representatives on behalf of the Klein group within the Independent Group. They sought and gained power within the Independent Group and the Society because they had Klein group backing within the British Society. This had an intimidating effect on those Independent Group analysts who wished to continue to think openly about their own tradition of thought.

Matters became so politicized that the works of Balint, Winnicott, Milner, and others became too politically risky to discuss, and the over-all effect was to stultify the tradition of thought that had constituted the Independent tradition.

This kind of intellectual rigidity is not uncommon at all in psycho-analytical training institutes. In the United States, for example, there are still reputable IPA institutes that do not teach the work of Melanie Klein or Winnicott; indeed, it would be considered a career risk for young analysts to mention them. Indeed, the British Society earned a some-what awestruck worldwide reputation for allowing the representation and discussion of intellectual differences, a situation that was true until the early 1970s but has not been true since.

It was not power politics alone, however, that led to the demise of the Independent Group thinkers. It was a failure to properly under-stand their task. While it was clear to the Klein group that their task was to understand the dynamics of the internal world and to analyse the varied representations of unconscious phantasy; while it was clear in the Anna Freud group that their task was to continue to refine Freud's metapsychology, linking it to the reality of the clinical encounter; the Independent Group seemed populated by gifted, off-beat writers, who had a penchant for plain English and an interest in idiosyncratic clinical encounters, but without a sufficiently articulate idea of which area of psychoanalysis they were addressing.

In my view, they were character analysts. One of the reasons they seemed so "impressionistic", "woolly", "unfocused", and "a-theoretical" was that they were trying to find a way to think about how one is affected by the other person's character. The impressions made by one character upon another are by definition imprecise, mutable, and idiomatic. Asked by Kleinians about what was going on in the patient's "internal world", or queried by Freudians about the metapsychological status of a presented patient, Independents seemed lost in the headlamps. Having failed to see their collective interest and task (character analysis), they could not respond to questions that came from entirely valid but utterly different categories than those presented by Independents.

The Independent Group of analysts had a long tradition from Jones and the Stracheys, from Sharpe and Richman, from Winnicott and Milner, from Khan and Klauber, from Michael and Enid Balint, Coltart and Stewart, from Padel and Tonnesmann, and others. This tradition is the subject of studies by Gregorio Kohon and Eric Rayner.[4]

By the early 1980s, however, the tradition of thought exemplified by a remarkable group of thinkers was in its dying days. The Independent was now the Middle Group and the project of thought that was associated with the names of Winnicott, Milner, and Balint had ceased to be supported within the Institute of Psychoanalysis. The British Psychoanalytical Society was now determined to settle on a neo-Kleinian orthodoxy that would be comfortable enough for all three groups to embrace. It would be a comfortable concept of the transference—sufficiently loosely formulated for the three groups to make their own particular version of it—that held that the bread and butter of psychoanalysis was what was going on between the patient and the analyst.

Jonathan Sklar studied psychiatry at Friern Barnet Hospital, The Whittington, The Royal Free Hospital, and at Halliwick Day Hospital, and gained his MRCPsych from the Royal College of Psychiatry. He trained in Psychotherapy in the Adult Department of the Tavistock Clinic while also undertaking psychoanalytical training at the Institute of Psychoanalysis in London. He was referred to Enid Balint for his training analysis, and he was supervised by Paula Heimann, Harold Stewart, and Pearl King.

One of the requirements of the Tavistock training was that trainees be attached to a GP surgery. Although Sklar writes about his work in what became known as Balint groups (in a follow-up volume to this book), mention needs to be made of what a remarkable step this was in the practice of medicine and psychotherapy. Through the work of Michael and Enid Balint and the next generation of clinicians—in particular Dr Sklar—ordinary doctors had psychoanalysts seconded to their clinics. Usually someone from the Tavistock would be attached to a clinic for a year or so, meeting patients who had emotional problems. There, they would receive assessments but also focal treatment if possible, and as the decades passed hundreds of ordinary doctors came into regular contact with psychoanalysts and psychotherapists. They saw before their eyes, so to speak, the profound impact of a clinical interview. Many of the patients seen by Balint group analysts were psychotic or had severely disturbed character disorders, and yet through psychotherapy there was clear therapeutic movement; indeed, so much so that generations of ordinary doctors did not reach for their medicine chests to prescribe psychotropic drugs.

At Halliwick Day Hospital, run by an eccentric genius, Dr Michael Conran, Dr Sklar ran the back wards populated by the most ill patients.

Later in his career, Dr Sklar would be Head of Psychotherapy at Cambridge Hospital in Cambridge, where he would continue to treat the severely ill and conduct seminars and workshops on psychopathology and the treatment of the psychoses.

As you will find in the chapters to follow, however, Dr Sklar saw severely disturbed analysands in private practice throughout his career. This also needs some explaining. It was considered ordinary for newly qualified psychoanalysts to take into five-times-weekly analysis severely disturbed people: from schizophrenics and manic depressives, to severe narcissistic personality disorders, malignant hysterics, and drug addicts. In those days, young analysts in Great Britain were learning from their patients (to allude to the work of the gifted Patrick Casement)[5] how to provide a psychoanalytic treatment for the schizophrenic or the manic depressive.

The writings of Balint, Winnicott, Milner, R. D. Laing, Rosenfeld, Rey, Bion, and Stewart were seminal texts in the exploration of how to work in this area, and the next generation of analysts would continue this tradition. Many would write about work in this area. As you read Dr Sklar's clinical accounts, which are to my mind unparalleled in their representation of the psychoanalysis of the deeply disturbed and regressed analysand, be reminded that Sklar's remit was a licence issued from the heart and soul of the British Psychoanalytical Society. If there were unfortunate political wars between the groups, there was unanimous consent that psychoanalysis should be available to anyone, no matter what they suffered, and that each person had the right to a psychoanalysis without being saturated in medication as a condition of treatment.

In addition, as Kohon[6] has pointed out, there was a long-standing tradition of admitting lay analysts to training; indeed, not only to the point where the difference between "medical or non-medical" all but vanished, but where the Admissions Committee of the Institute vigorously sought candidates from anthropology, literature, philosophy, business … and the world of sport! Such academic open-mindedness also went hand in hand with a silent commitment to social democracy: people were regularly offered five-times-a-week analysis for far less than a North American analyst would make in a single hour. Working-class and lower-middle-class patients were seen at the London Clinic of Psychoanalysis and also by senior analysts, enabling British clinicians the opportunity to work with severely disturbed analysands, many of whom were incapable of employment. These were the patients who in

North America were placed for the most part on life-long medications, depriving North American psychoanalysis of valuable experience of regular contact with psychotic and severely disturbed analysands in medication-free psychoanalysis.

There are many gifted writers who still follow the Independent line of thought, even if the group exists in name only. Michael Parson's[7] elegant and thoughtful essays, Roger Kennedy's straightforward, lucid credo,[8] and Gregorio Kohon's[9] integrative texts are all vital contributions in keeping the torch alive. Sklar's book will be in that tradition, but with a twist. He manages to write up work with the severely disturbed patient in a way that is unsurpassed by the new generation of analytical writers. If he is to be likened to anyone from the previous generation, I think it must be Nina Coltart, who hewed her essays from very specific clinical encounters.

As you read Dr Sklar, remember, he does not presume to represent psychoanalysis. He does not even represent the range of his own practice. He is concentrating in these writings on conveying what it is like to work with analysands whose trauma has been from the Real, who present their disturbances in the relationship to the psychoanalyst, who must feel his way through the many impressions of sessions towards the construction of a transformative history.

This is a work on character analysis.

And Sklar's literary character is in this text, as you will see. This is a work that owes a huge debt to Ferenczi and Balint, of whose tradition Sklar is a direct heir. It also reveals his overdetermination by his remarkable colleagues in the British Psychoanalytical Society.

Endnotes

1. See *The Freud–Klein Controversies 1941–1945*, edited by Pearl King and Riccardo Steiner (London: Tavistock/Routledge, 1991).
2. Personal communication.
3. Each group—Kleinian, Independent, Freudian—had their own individual group meetings, usually once every two months or so. Sometimes, a member would present a paper, at other times the entire group would have an open discussion on a clinical issue, and increasingly in the Independent Group in the 1980s, the group was concerned with its identity.

4. See *The British School of Psychoanalysis: The Independent Tradition*, edited by Gregorio Kohon (London: Free Association, 1986) and *The Independent Mind in British Psychoanalysis*, edited by Eric Rayner (London: Free Association, 1990).

5. See *On Learning from the Patient* by Patrick Casement (London: Tavistock, 1985).

6. See *The British School of Psychoanalysis: The Independent Tradition*.

7. See *The Dove that Returns the Dove that Vanishes* (London and Philadelphia: Routledge, 2000).

8. See *Freedom to Relate* (London: Free Association, 1993).

9. See *No Lost Certainties To Be Recovered* (London: Karnac Books, 1999).

CHAPTER ONE

The rebirth of history and trauma in psychoanalysis

She gathered up all the fragments
But could not make them fit.

Anna Akhmatova (1912, p. 100)

T
he papers contained in this volume span some twenty-five years'
practice in psychoanalysis. They are written from the point of
view of a psychoanalyst nurtured within the British Society and,
in particular, the Independent tradition that stretches back to the clinical and theoretical dialogues of Freud and Ferenczi through Winnicott
and Michael and Enid Balint towards the twenty-first century. During
this time, the British Psychoanalytical Society has moved from being a
Society of three theoretical strands comprising the Independent, Contemporary Freudian, and Kleinian groups to one that has given up
the "gentleman's agreement" in order to be one group in one Society.
Presently, education in the Institute is suffused with a surfeit of "here
and now" analysis with a considerable loss of analytic interest in free
association and history. The atmosphere is now one in which a senior analyst in the Society can state, "I have come to bury Free Association not to praise it" (McDermott 2003, pp. 1349–1356) without

1

inhibition or concern for the historical part played by that concept in the development of psychoanalysis. Often, the main focus is on the manifest content of clinical material rather than what lies behind the surface—the depth of the latent unconscious meanings of the dream and the meanderings of free association in the clinical work. The papers in this volume highlight the value and everyday use of history in order to retrieve analytic traditions which, like that of free association, have been pushed aside.

Psychoanalysts in clinical practice usually have curiosity about things discarded, killed, and buried. Freud described with clarity in his *A Note Upon the "Mystic Writing-Pad"* (Freud 1925) how experiences of events and of feelings about relationships are etched on the unconscious and how, as they pass from the present into the day residues and then to one's personal unconscious history, they can exert a presence, even if apparently absent from everyday life. For some severe early traumas, the etching of its representations may be disrupted if the unconscious substrate is itself subject to a process of defensive fragmentation. This makes its conscious recapture particularly difficult, and requires a form of analysis that looks more to being within the experience and its associated affects than just a process of intellectual understanding. Only a wakening of lost affect is potentially able to connect deep splits in the ego.

We will also look back historically to other matters etched in the historical development of psychoanalysis as a subject. In particular, to the consequences of Ferenczi's famous 1933 paper "Confusion of Tongues", where he is concerned about whose agenda is being examined, who is talking to whom, and the ensuing disagreements in the relationship between Freud and Ferenczi. Essentially the argument between them was about theory and technique, and in particular how the analysand could at times be stuck despite all interpretative attempts in the analysis. The subject of the child in the adult during the analytic encounter was of much interest to Ferenczi, especially the level of what was being communicated in the present about an earlier voice (Ferenczi 1931). Faced with such a clinical situation, Ferenczi realized the profound relevance of enactment, found in the consulting room, which he came to understand and discover was invariably some fragment often revoked and disguised from an earlier traumatic position. This became a pointer to the ways such an impasse could develop. The background to their difference was that Ferenczi thought that as well as unconscious phantasy there were the actual experiences that had happened that could profoundly matter. To make matters more complex, early traumatic experiences were also fertile soil for the development of unconscious phantasy, but the importance was that they were rooted in an actual experience or, more commonly, gathered into what Khan described as "cumulative trauma" (Khan 1963, p. 46). For Freud, however, it was as if Ferenczi was signalling a wholesale retreat to theory prior to the Oedipus complex. Ferenczi recognized the links between the two stages of Freud's early theory; initially one of infantile seduction, and then later Freud's discovery of the ubiquity of the Oedipus complex as an unconscious mental structure. Ferenczi discovered the profound interdependence of real early experiences together with the Oedipus complex rather than one theory supplanting the other. Ferenczi found that many patients (later he would state all, see Ferenczi & Freud 1920–1933, p. 376) had indeed suffered much early trauma of one sort or another. This was often "found" as fixity in the analysis; an unconscious repetition or in the refinding of the analysand's personal history that was unconsciously enacted as the only way of discovery, unavailable to be spoken as a known thing in a more straightforward classically analytic way. In a sense, the actualization of the fixed moment is part of transference, the difference being that it required being experienced rather than just known intellectually. The refinding of experience in the consulting room then becomes, as we shall see in the clinical accounts in the chapters that follow, the harbinger of affect and aliveness which can enable the analysis to move on.

Ferenczi added an additional level of complexity whilst being unafraid to acknowledge the implications of his position in the context of the transference–countertransference. A move away from the past, reconstruction and free association can lead the young analyst trained to continually notice and address all surface phenomena as a commentary on the analyst–analysand relationship, to suggest that this can be the sole basis for knowing a truth because one is there at the time of its making. This is a considerable move away from connecting with unconscious life. Such forms of analysis stay far from a need for reconstruction. We need to remember that Freud returns to the value of reconstruction in analysis at the end of his writings (Freud 1938). Despite the special status afforded to transference, Freud also writes:

> The patient cannot remember the whole of what is repressed in him, and what he cannot remember may be precisely the

essential part of it. He is obliged to *repeat* the repressed material as a contemporary experience, instead of, as the physician would prefer to see, *remembering* it as something belonging to the past.

(Freud 1920, p. 18)

The Freudian position, elaborated over a long period, is designed to allow the analyst to utilize himself as a working instrument in touch with his own unconscious mind in relation to the unconscious mind of the patient. The analyst's unconscious is working with the free associations of the patient. As associations are free, sentences can move in many directions and, if left alone, the patient usually settles on an area of thought that both patient and analyst may be surprised to find. Finding oneself in such unexpected landscapes can be profound. Such moments resonate with unconscious connection, facilitating deepening understanding. It can lead to a greater sense of ownership, instead of "ideas given by the analyst".

After all, classic analysis teaches that analysis works by utilizing the unconscious communication of the analytic dyad. If the analyst is looking out for specific phenomena, in order to support the analyst's own theory, then the analysis will not be free to roam wherever, whether consciously or unconsciously. Perhaps analysts have to realize that at times, their own desire for a particular piece of analytic theory is due to an area of their own unique object-relations system, or even their own pathology. Knowing such matters helps the analyst's development of free-floating attention a great deal. Yet this is somewhat different from expecting an analytic line, to the exclusion of other tracks. The patient will often avail himself or herself of analyst's perception of the elements of the material which they have highlighted and enjoyed as a form of compliance. A common example occurs on a weekly basis when the analyst interprets the impact of the impending weekend gap and underlines it at the following Monday session as if this must be the most important dynamic for the patient. This interpretative line may be heard by the analysand as the narcissism of the analyst who always puts himself in the position of being missed. Many trainees quickly learn how to incorporate such technique, which is a process similar to the patient learning the analyst's rules and desires. In this model, the imaginative life pursued by the analysand at the weekend appears less interesting. Not surprisingly, anger and dismay may emerge when colleagues challenge such a view, as such assertions have far wider implications than disagreements about the detail of clinical material and its meanings. Rather, such a challenge directs attention towards the entire focus underpinning that particular technique, implying that it has moved away from the unconscious, the body ego, and sexuality by relinquishing Freud's great instrument "free association". Nowadays, even dream analysis has been re-thought as pertaining more to the here and now of the manifest content than as a process whose importance is to sink into a more unfamiliar and dangerous unknown latent world.

In his book on Jewish memory, the distinguished scholar Yosef Hayim Yerushalmi writes: "A concern with history is not an innate endowment of human civilisation" (Yerushalmi 1982, p. 6). Many cultures, he notes, have found no virtue in the historical dimension of human existence. Instead, primitive societies endowed "mythic rather than historical time as 'real', the time of primeval beginnings and paradigmatic first acts, the dream time when the world was new, suffering unknown, and men consorted with the gods" (ibid.). This might be one way of approaching Freud's famous shift from real event to phantasy: his discovery of the Oedipal myth that seemed to usurp his earlier idea that the neurotic had been subject to abuse, seduction, or physical harm. In this book, I argue that we need to hold on to both of these insights, both forms of time—historical and mythic—to seize the complex psychic temporality of the patient and of the analytic relation. Alongside the key emphasis on phantasy, I believe that psychoanalysis must also hover around the possibility of re-finding such primitive beginnings and is sorely lightened if the focus remains in a one-time dimension of the present. It can be argued that the seeds of our life are sown by the reality of early experiences which can be modulated, for better or worse, by the environment. The title of one of Winnicott's books is *The Maturational Processes and the Facilitating Environment* (Winnicott 1965), which expresses very well the idea that internal unconscious representations have a relationship with external objects such as the mother in pre-birth and early life, and that the real experiences garnered by the infant acquire depth and meaning in that period, as well as later on. I will be writing about the specificity of interpretation, but in the environment of the analytic process. In time, the introjection of this external environment becomes essential new internal space.

It was actually as a Freudian that Ferenczi wanted to maintain the two positions, holding on to the mythic element while also keeping open the possibility that something may have happened in historical reality. To make matters even more complex, the clinical structure must also allow for the *après coup*: the perception of knowledge altering in the unconscious. This comprehension, held by many within the Independent tradition, allows for an understanding of complex layerings of history, including history altered by *après coup*, as a means of understanding the life of the analysand in the present tense. In this tradition, instead of seeing an historical state of mind as analytically unclear and therefore suspect, the possibility of thinking and feeling about history is valued, whether it is an actual fact or nuanced within complex unconscious imaginings. All the essays that follow are written in light of this complex dual insight.

The Independent analyst Phil Mollon has recently written about transference as presently understood in a lighter, more surface, way. He writes:

> The "modern view" of many British analysts is remote from Freud's concept of transference as "false connection", or misperception in which "what appears to be reality is in fact only a portion of a forgotten past"—a misperception or illusion that is "constantly destroyed" by the work of analysis.
>
> (Mollon 2009, p. 26)

He continues:

> If "transference" is now seen merely as the continual expression of the patient's object relational world in relation to the analyst, rather than as a more occasional emergence of a "forgotten past", then it would follow that there is nothing other than transference to address—indeed nowhere else to go and nothing else to talk about. There is no intrusion of past into the present, no penetration of unconscious contents into the preconscious, and no viable distinction between transference and the real relationship. However, the cost of this modern perspective is that the Freudian transference of "false connection" and "misalliance" is foreclosed—excluded from contemporary discourse, along with the original focus on reconstruction. From a Freudian perspective interpretation of transference and reconstruction of the developmental past go hand in

hand, two sides of the same technical coin—each informing the other and neither making much sense without the other. It is a matter of reworking the past through its transference into the present, but depending crucially upon continually dissolving the illusion by means of identifying its source in the developmental past.

(ibid., p. 207)

In tune with my emphasis here, Mollon is arguing for the complexity of the analytic process, rather than working in a more surface way, which narrows the possibilities of understanding and communication by being only in the present in the clinical session. In such a view, there is no multiplicity of paths to follow. It is unsurprising to find that this "here and now" way of working has a following amongst young analysts, as sessions are easier to think and predict. There is less possibility of the analyst becoming lost in the material or finding it hard to give weight to one of numerous associative pathways. Instead of accepting the fate of not knowing at a given moment in the session, the easier tendency is to prefer "knowing". In this state, the analyst can hold on to an intellectual handle and this may feel more comfortable, and as a good position for the analyst to hold. This contrasts, in my opinion, with the ideas put forward in these essays that psychoanalysis works by disturbance, by finding the unexpected, and by allowing that the analysand will be closely examining how the analyst is able to deal or not deal with what is happening. My use of the word "allowing" is deliberate and is a different idea from understanding. It describes being in the moment with the analysand, rather than being directed by or done to, as a different experience. Being in the emotional experience in a moment of the material is considerably different from only noticing the transference in the manifest material and from an external position. It is a state of analytic acceptance that one is working in the dark.

* * *

This understanding of psychoanalytic practice finds its expression in these essays in relation to a specific set of clinical preoccupations which have in turn played a key role in its conceptualization. The patient, as Winnicott put it, can teach the analyst. Regression, the psyche-soma, and various ways of understanding the complexities of trauma are the central concerns of this book. All of these concepts offer new opportunities to articulate the relationship between history and the unconscious. The clinical focus is slanted towards the analysis of some severely ill people who have unconsciously had to develop psychotic, addictive, or psychosomatic strategies in order to survive. These strategies have the profoundest implications for the question of analytic technique. What we then clearly see again is that the original ego is a body ego. By this, I mean that early on in the development of the mind, the ego has perceptions from the body, for instance posture, hunger, pain, cold, and heat. These are experiences in the body prior to and later alongside the development of a thinking–feeling mechanism. It is the analysand's body that provides the structure and motility to bring the mind to analysis. To examine thought processes in analysis while at the same time noticing the body in the consulting room leads, of course, to further complexity. The mind does not exist without its body and both structures, consciously and unconsciously, in all their complex dynamic, have been around for the duration of that person's life. In my view, present-day analysis can often relegate the value and importance of the body as part of the totality of analytic experience. At its most extreme, the mind becomes overvalued as the target organ for some analysts. The analytic understanding of psyche-soma can become an ordinary, but also fundamental, way of understanding and approaching the roots of an individual's character or self. After all, attendance for a session can only happen by the body bringing itself to the analyst.

Freud's paper *Neurosis and Psychosis* (1924) is seminal for the way it allows us to understand not just the notion of a gap in the ego, but the struggle by the unconscious to make good the gap and to attempt repair: "In regard to the genesis of delusions", writes Freud, "a fair number of analyses have taught us that the delusion is found applied like a patch over the place where originally a rent had appeared in the ego's relation to the external world" (Freud 1924, p. 151). The gap, in time, can become the "split" in the ego. However, this is more complicated than it seems, as the German for "split" is *Einreiss*, which leans more to a meaning of a "tendency to tear". This throws another perspective on to Freud's meaning because a "tendency" includes the idea that despite being fragile, the tear may not worsen. It is not a break. This is less critical than a *Reiss*, which is an actual tear and is more a term to delegate to psychosis (Danckwardt & Wegner 2007, p. 1118). This is the first recognition by Freud that the ego itself can be ill rather than healthy, being unable to stave off the other agencies of the mind. The split in the ego can mean that things are both really known and quite unknown simultaneously, like a life lived in a concurrent parallel way. Intellectually, one might prefer to think that if a person knows one and the other in parallel, then both states are known and the one knows the other, as it were. In severe mental illness, this is often not at all true. In addition, a sense of persecution from the tear in the mind can exist beneath the patch which is designed to cover it up. An *Einreiss* moving to a *Reiss* really does mean a deep gap between a mind knowing things on one side of the canyon but hardly, if at all, beyond on the other side. The patch covering the tear in the mind like a dream is a symptom that attempts reconnection with reality. That *"which we take to be the pathological product, is in reality an attempt at recovery, a process of reconstruction"* writes Freud (1911, p. 71, italics in original). As Danckwardt and Wegner note: "The patient must keep himself from knowing that because of the disruption caused by the tormenting certainty of being persecuted, the effectiveness of his own attempt at cure, which was his auto therapeutic response to the illness, is denied to him" (Danckwardt & Wegner 2007, p. 1119).

In his 1924 paper *Neurosis and Psychosis*, Freud highlighted the delusion as a patch, thereby directing attention to the delusions, imaginary constructs, as well as fixities of the body (such as a patient to be discussed with a diagnosis of spasmodic torticollis), that enable life apparently to continue on the surface as if there is no mental gap or tear. The symptoms are there as a covering structure to enable some sense of not fragmenting. The patch over the ego does not have a healing function, it is an unconscious phantasy because the deeper mental structures held apart from each other do not grow together. Instead, the patch can become more organized, such as a delusional system quietly enlarging to take account of the different unconscious narratives and relational affects on either side of the tear. Like dreams, this image of patchwork, if taken seriously, can become another royal road to understanding unconscious process through which the healing of deep splits, albeit with psychic scars, can occur. The clinical importance of such a stance is considerable. Instead of the patient experiencing constant disruption around the gap, whenever reality inevitably intrudes on the individual, as he vainly attempts to keep both parts of the mind apart, a mental scar formation can take place as a form of repair. This allows the patient to bear their suffering with less need for the symptoms mounting a defence of the split in the mind and its associated attack on external reality.

It is here that we need once more to turn to Ferenczi who, with his pupil Michael Balint, was greatly interested in the treatment of severely ill patients. For both, regression was an essential concept, as a way to begin to describe the process of going back in time in order to know more about present predicaments. The patient, in a state of regression, was inside an experience that was, in certain meaningful ways, a re-experience—of atmospheres and affects from early object relationships. The clinical practice of regression allowed Ferenczi to conceptualize an understanding of early mental assault, which could lead, in his view, to the "defensive atomization" of mental structures. By means of this idea, Ferenczi was trying to examine the little that might be available to the ego when pathological splitting processes are unable to contain the depth of intellectual and emotional dissonance, invariably around the issues of life and death, suicide and murder, and the horror of what people can do to one another, especially between adults and children. This is a theory about the roots of trauma and its effects on the early development of mind. It is important to consider that the need for some patients to deeply regress in analysis, is viewed by many analysts as something to avoid. For many analysts, the concept of regression has also been buried. Analytic work utilizing states of regression is often regarded as antithetical and schematic. In relation to a sense of analytic fixity, Laplanche and Pontalis write: "In so far as fixation is to be understood as an 'inscription' regression might be interpreted as the bringing back into play of what had been 'inscribed'" (Laplanche & Pontalis 1973, p. 388). If the analyst is able to realize that regression is not such a dangerous activity, it may usefully be brought back into play. Meaning the use of play is a creative experience away from being in a state of paranoia that dictates that play is potentially dangerous and must be avoided.

Freud's and Ferenczi's concepts of regression are, however, very different. For Freud, regression needed to be understood and primarily interpreted, but for Ferenczi, the emphasis in addition was on the idiom of the experience: "It definitely looks", he wrote in 1912, "as if one could never reach any real convictions at all through logical insight alone; one needs to have lived through an affective experience, to have so to speak, felt it in one's body, in order to gain conviction" (Ferenczi 1912, pp. 193–194). He believed that action and acting out were not necessarily defensive or about resistance. Instead, in line with Freud in *Remembering, Repeating and Working-Through* (Freud 1914), he thought that through reliving an experience, repetition was transformed into remembering, leading to knowledge.

This theoretical and clinical orientation towards experience in the analytic setting is continued in the work of Balint and Winnicott. Thus Balint's concept of a "new beginning" came directly out of Ferenczi's 1928 idea of "the elasticity of psychoanalytic technique" in which the tension between the analytic dyad is a pull between one and the other, often unconsciously including, or even re-enacting, the split in the patient's mind (Ferenczi 1955). Of critical importance is the analyst's own authenticity. It is the atmosphere of analytic authenticity that the analysand invariably does not expect to find and for the more seriously ill it is a near unknown luxury whose very possibility promotes destructive paranoia over long periods of time, as its very existence in a new relationship is too upsetting in relation to known life. As a concept, the new beginning is a way of taking the split in the ego seriously and attempting its closure, which will have profound effects on unconscious internal object relationships. An example of inauthentic analytic experience would be patients who speak and receive in return a textbook interpretation as a learned response from the analyst. Lost in the middle of a complex session, the analyst may want to reach into a theoretical catch-all based on learned response. Such an activity may feel more comfortable for the analyst. This could be perceived as analyst-centred, the interpretation having been drawn from a theoretical position of the analyst rather than coming out of an unconscious listening and waiting for meaning to emerge. It is considerably harder for the analyst to maintain silence, to sustain a position of not knowing rather than needing to say something. It might even be that the speech act is only meaningful as a way of the analyst keeping himself alive at a particular moment. This in itself may be important not just for the analyst, as a way of warding off his own internal despair, but also for the analysand to unconsciously notice that the analyst is in the room and they are not alone. But at such a moment, what may matter more is the form of attention rather than the content of the analyst's words.

A central analytic question therefore becomes whether there are one or two people in the consulting room. Ferenczi felt the need to discover techniques in order both to understand and, more importantly clinically, to connect emotionally with some patients who have spent their lives protecting themselves by existing without the other. A solipsistic life by its very nature protects the self and the other from (further) acts of destructiveness. At the same time, much of the emotional and relational richness of the external world is killed in the thin life led. Some patients may appear on the surface to live a life in the context of others, but actually are all alone. It can appear in the consulting room as if two persons are present, yet in time the analyst is forced to recognize that he may not be, or may not be allowed to be, psychically present for his patient. This would be a description of John Rickman's one-person psychology: "One-person psychology concerns itself with what goes on inside one person taken in isolation" (Rickman 1957, p. 218). It is not a relationship of reciprocity that can be discovered in two-person psychology. Highly influential in the 1950s, although probably less well known these days, Rickman had left London for Vienna in 1920 to be analysed by Freud. The importance of his observation is that if interpretations are directed Oedipally or in the transference towards the dyadic relationship of analyst–analysand, as if it is obvious that two persons are present, then, unsurprisingly, they will flounder unheard if they are directed at the patient who, at that moment, is alone only with himself in the consulting room.[1]

In the psychotic arena, which is repeatedly my focus in this book, patients may not be able to hear and accept interpretation, digest and work it through. The patients may not know that another person is even in the room with them. The analyst's sentences and interpretations might be heard, not as words, but as things, and we might recall here Freud's famous differentiation between word presentation and thing presentation (Freud 1915). When the analyst does speak, the patient may perceive the sentence as a device to penetrate. Immense care must be taken in trying to imagine or envisage, for instance, which part of the body receives the interpretation when the patient is in a state of pathological regression. As Ernest Jones showed, words are not necessarily received into the ears, but can be felt as entering another body space, with all its concomitant imaginary dangers (Jones 1951). Words at times contain the capacity to be experienced physically in the body as seduction or aggression.

* * *

Several of my clinical examples describe the near impossibility of reaching an analysand who has almost given up the concept or possibility of being found by another. Such is the life of patients who find a way of clinging to a marginal life through psychotic mechanisms, such as delusional thought, or drug-induced aloneness, or who retreat into somatization. In all such clinical encounters, the movement from the solipsistic world to a two-person relationship, which implies transference and the possibility of re-finding the Oedipal world of three persons (infant, mother, and father) becomes available only by registering an antecedent traumatic landscape. This is often deeply buried or hidden beneath the surface with possibly all traces kicked over.

Winnicott can help us here in understanding such processes. He postulated a process in which something was actually seen by the child, something so awful that it led to a de-hallucination in which it was covered over. Subsequently, a series of hallucinations begins to fill up the hole produced by the scotomization. Winnicott described watching a child paint a picture using bright colours to portray a lively scene. This was quickly followed by the child finding the black paint and carefully and completely covering the first scene, wiping out the earlier representation. If one had not observed the beginning, then one would be left to speculate only about the blackness. He described such a process as compulsive in that it had to be repeated again and again.

This slight example also reveals the importance of keeping the mind open to an historical line of enquiry, for without such a capacity, it is easy to promote the idea that the child's black picture is a representation of the death instinct. Clearly, these representations, layered one on top of the other, convey a much more complex picture. We see something related in the transference when some patients need to be psychotic in order to arrive at memories of a very disturbed and distressing kind belonging to an earlier time. Like the black paint of the child, psychosis is a representation of the dark landscape concealing (and pointing towards) early severe trauma. Hallucinations are a form of creative life. Winnicott's observation also contains the idea that it is the patient who now has the desire and capacity to "black" something. Now the past and the present reach a fusion that requires analysis to untangle the original "black" that assaulted the child and their own identification with a blackening/blanking out that is both self-protective and also an attack on the object. Any affect is projected onto the surface of the picture, in the flatness of the colour, black covering the other pigments and far from the internal feelings of affect. By becoming an artist, the damaged child is unconsciously attempting to find a new location for a description of the trauma on paper as a picture or poem, which can thus be externalized. We should not be misled, however, into thinking that such transcription can be consciously understood by the patient as an important retrieval of early life. As with painting, the process is more tentative. Good-enough art has the capacity to allow the viewer to be unconsciously in touch with something of the poignancy of this early unconscious human situation.

In each of these cases, something unbearable is struggling for representation. If Ferenczi is also important here, it is because he was particularly interested in finding the balance between fantasy and trauma. "In all cases in which I have penetrated deeply enough", he wrote to Freud on 25 December 1929:

> I found the traumatic-hysterical basis for the illness [...] The critical view that gradually formed in me in the process was that psychoanalysis engages too much one-sidedly in obsessional neurosis and character analysis i.e., ego psychology, neglecting the organic hysterical basis for the analysis; the cause lies in the over estimation of fantasy and the under estimation of traumatic reality in pathogenesis.
>
> (Ferenczi & Freud 1920–1933, p. 376)

Similarly, in my clinical work, it is the gradual or, in some cases, sudden and unexpected tripping over traumatic memories that can bring the analysis to life. The difficulty in this area is that the return of the repressed trauma can become diffused into the transference–countertransference. It is likely that a sudden violent aggression can erupt, such as the patient coming close to attacking themselves (usually again) and/or perceiving the analyst as perpetrator, and hence repeater, of the original sense of trauma experienced by the patient. Of course, such moments can signal an imminent assault on the analyst: in Chapter Four, we will visit and discuss such an analytic scene.

For Ferenczi, at times this was unavoidable. "I have come to realize", he wrote in his diary on 8 March 1932, "that it is an unavoidable task for the analyst: although he may behave as he will, he may take kindness and relaxation as far as he possibly can, the time will come when he will have to repeat with his own hands the act of murder previously perpetrated against the patient" (Ferenczi 1988, p. 52).

The analyst therefore has to bear being the attacker, even the murderer, in the transference. He has to be able to work on such material, intermingling present and past, without the patient being too overwhelmed by their paranoia. For that matter, the analyst needs also not to be too overwhelmed by the authenticity of the part he has to bear. The capacity to work, in such a clinically restricted area, to both understand and to survive it, is the prelude to Balint's concept of new beginning. It is a matter of finding a way of getting beneath the blackness, which may appear as emptiness or an evacuated state of the patient. Otherwise, it is all too easy for the analyst to assume that the blackness is a bedrock and from there to make the case for negative therapeutic reaction. This may then trigger the sudden departure of the patient, leaving intact the analyst's unassailable sense that the patient was unanalysable! Unfortunately, such a position often simply allows the analyst not to understand what has suddenly happened and to protect the analyst from criticism, his own as well as others'.

In the area of object relating, Winnicott later theorized in a similar way. "After the subject relates to object comes subject destroys object and then may come object survives destruction by the subject" (Winnicott 1971, p. 90). Sometimes, after this, he continued, the object can be loved. Winnicott does not quote Ferenczi, but the two share a belief in the importance of surviving being killed in the transference, which implies that the analyst must be available for such death. Once he survives, the patient, invariably astonished, can begin to know about the usefulness of being able to love. It is the capacity to love that is so strikingly absent when such ill patients first arrive in the consulting room, not that it is even something to be considered or even complained about. This capacity to love also needs to include loving with ambivalence. Ambivalence allows hatred of the object.

Such thoughts take us deep down the pathological splits in the ego of the patient. At a deep unconscious level, the analyst in such cases is inevitably not just the container of the assaults, both real and imaginary, experienced earlier in the patient's life, but is unconsciously expected to actualize them again for the patient. As Freud pointed out, the finding of an object is always a re-finding (Freud 1905, p. 222).

Paula Heimann provided me with a poignant example via a personal communication. Her doorbell was once rung by a person who had no appointment with her. She decided to see the woman, who proceeded to relate her mental dysfunction to the fact of her parents having been in concentration camps with her as a young child. Having herself fled from Germany, Heimann knew that at times in the treatment of this young woman, the analyst would have no choice in the transference other than to be the death-giving Nazi. She also knew that, despite the horror which that structure held for her personally, she could not turn away the request for treatment. The analyst working with such clinical dysfunction knows that much of the work of transference and counter-transference will have to take place within such a structure of horror. Her example is a powerful instance, perhaps the exemplary instance for our times, of the question of survival in the analytic setting touched on so boldly by Ferenczi and Winnicott.

With such ill patients, interpretation can only be of use later in the analytic work when the analysand has dared, as it were (we could also call this "developed"), to notice the other in the room. The very regressed patient needs to deal with life by having very little of it. One way of dealing with profound early traumas is to close down much of oneself in order to provide as small a target as possible for the expectation of further mental and physical assault. Analysis then is a provision of a space and an environment for the possibility of a return to life. The depth of trauma can be registered by the amount of empty time required for such a character to dare to seek an object again. This can be an act of considerable bravery for the analysand who has to re-find traumatic moments that have been effectively repressed, split off, or somatized. Prior to such a return to hope, the analysand has first to find a creative part of himself as a form of becoming alive. I am thinking of the capacity of the artist to articulate and reframe his pain and realization of, say, early abandonment by finding an ability to play with paint as a way of returning to the possibilities inherent in child's play. Such matters may go on separately to the analysis, which, in itself, might seem empty and sterile for long periods of time. The analyst needs to be patient, and not misread such moments of stasis as negative transference or refusal of the analytic process. In fact, the work, enabled by the treatment, might be going on elsewhere.

* * *

Traumatized patients have often developed exquisite sensibilities, the capacity to take in with a brief glance, or by sniffing the atmosphere in the consulting room, the very essence of earlier figures that were required to be more important than them. One might then think that a point of transference has entered the scene. Yet an interpretation of the transference position, as perceived by the analyst, may not be heard. Further interpretation about the destruction evoked by ignoring the analyst may only drive the analysandfurther into being alone or require a defensive false acceptance. When the analyst later realizes the superficiality of the position, he can be plunged into a depression, which is often projected onto the patient as a negative therapeutic reaction.

I work from a position that such patients can only find their way to the analyst in their own time and, often, with their own interpretation. For some analysands, everything that had been offered from the early carers was so tainted with self-serving that they have developed a form of primitive knowledge or impulse to accept nothing from the other. Technically, one needs to wait without despair. Words may become things that intrude. Ideas from without may then invade and disrupt. External reason is felt as an attack. The patient is in an unreachable place, yet knowing, despite all else, that the patient daily attends their analysis, can be a hopeful sign for the analyst. That in itself is a great deal and can be a form of silent participation by just being there.

This can be a most unusual experience for the very ill patient, who has been filled with an earlier knowledge of what the other wants for himself. Michael Balint described an "Area of Basic Fault" where the patient is silent, lifeless, and hopeless. Such a phase, Enid Balint later elaborated,

> is only overcome when this phase is worked through, that is, when the patient is no longer regressed to a stage where he has no mutual experience with his analyst but becomes silently hostile, disillusioned and desperate and eventually appears to give up hope. He sometimes does this without reproaching the analyst, who may wonder what he is doing wrong. ... This state is overcome only when the patient painfully allows himself to feel alone, in the analyst's presence but with no person being there. He may then begin to perceive for himself and to enter the Area of Creativity. The patient is alone with no other person present, but the space is not empty. There is no experience of a void and the analytic hour is in fact a relief from the previous experience of compliance.

> (E. Balint 1993, pp. 104–105)

For Enid Balint, entering a creativeness alone in the presence of the other is the direction of the analytic journey and has to occur prior to the patient recognizing the meaning of the two-person relationship.

This does not mean that the relationship has not been noticed, rather that it is not perceived as important. It only becomes so when it matures into a two-person relationship which must include, at times, the painful realization of absence. At such a time, creative play, like thumb-sucking, is recognized as not providing the real thing. Realizing the loss of the other becomes a later and nonetheless crucial experience on the developmental path. It includes the desire for the lost object, no longer in the realms of a return to a damaging sadomasochistic experience, but in the form of a new experience gradually built on trust and concern. That this is not a falsely positive vision is clear from Winnicott's insistence on destruction and survival as an inherent part of the process. Such states of mind contain paradoxes: "At the start is an essential aloneness. At the same time this aloneness can only take place under maximum conditions of dependence" (Winnicott 1988, p. 132).

Likewise, Christopher Bollas eloquently describes the mutuality, at times, of the destructive process as an essential component to being alive: "The analyst destroys the patient's manifest texts in order to reveal unconscious meanings and the patient destroys the analyst through that particular object usage we call transference" (Bollas 1989, p. 36). "I suggest", he continues,

> that for a good destruction of the analyst to take place, one that is not constituted out of the death instinct but is part of the life instinct, the analyst must indicate to the patient, at the right moment, that he is ready for destruction. The "to be destroyed" analyst has a different function—indeed is a different object—from that analyst who deconstructs the material.
>
> (ibid., p. 36)

If this seems somewhat formalized as something known that will occur during a moment in a session, in my experience it is rather some place or atmosphere that one unwittingly finds oneself in—a cold, horrible, unfriendly, and frankly dangerous dark landscape.

When working with severely damaged patients, such moments are far more than elegiac—far more than a countertransferential invitation for the analyst to enter the experience of the analysand, all those years ago, in order to have some emotional being-in-the-moment of what it may have felt like then. Rather, or in addition to this, it feels as if the analyst's capacity to imagine that he can do analytic work is being destroyed. In fact, the patient is directing unconscious attention to a rock bottom to see if, in the midst of such experience, the analyst is still alive.

In this context, an analyst too preoccupied with himself, with having an effect or being able to get in touch with his patient, may well be perceived as being narcissistic and selfish. Many writings on Kleinian technique describe the analyst "showing the patient" such and such a fact (Joseph 1989). Some analysts have described in detail how the patient often attempts to draw them into forms of enactment that function as complex defensive organizations to preserve or restore a form of psychic equilibrium that protects the analysand from anxiety. In such a context, telling the patient a fact is intended to break through the defence. But the patient who is being told something in this way may have experienced many years of "being told" things, so the analyst's words risk an enactment of a previous overbearing parental position, with the analysand receiving knowledge from the one who knows, whose authority bears down on him, as before, from the outside world.

Contrast this with the Independent tradition's theory of being alongside and waiting with the analysand, so as quietly to differentiate the analytic process from an earlier power-centric model—a theory attacked in London for decades as being "wishy-washy", with no regard to the subtlety of the analytic stance. For many analysts, history is so distortable as to be unreliable compared with the present tense of the session. But this makes it harder to notice, even less theorize, their own dynamics of power, and in particular those moments when the analyst, by being in charge, may be unconsciously evoking a re-enactment of history. In such circumstances, the patient is likely to learn what the powerful analyst demands of him. Weekends may be perceived as special for the analyst who is preoccupied in restating their analytic significance and the patient may start to learn to comply with unspoken imaginary "rules" as a protective device. And what of the possibilities of the analyst's unconscious representation of earlier power plays in the life of the analysand?

Many analysts today are mistrustful of the concept of enactment, seeing it as a means for the patient to draw the analyst into acting out and therefore as strengthening the patient's defences. It is as if the patient desires only to wrong foot the analyst and attack analysis. This is very different to the idea that enactment might be a way, or even the only way sometimes, of retrieving past object states. Even if the analyst does allow that a certain degree of his own acting out may be inevitable, such a recognition serves to secure the analyst at a distance, trying to be aware, as an external and rational observer. This is far from the analyst described by Michael Balint, caught in an interpenetrating mix-up, who needs to be experienced as malignant before being found as "harmonious" with the patient.

In fact, beyond words, or unconscious things that are not yet able to be put into word form, enactment, as a process, can move the analysis forward so that meaning and affect and words can be found as new development. Despite concern that defences will be strengthened in states of regression, enactment can be another royal road to understanding of primitive object states. These primitive states, fixed in early trauma beyond words, can develop through to a new beginning as the analysand comes to be understood in the context of a holding environment. In the Independent tradition, the negative is used and is perceived less as antagonistic to the direction of therapeutics and without necessarily indicating an attack on analysis. Surely, if enactment is inevitable, this could lead the analyst to draw a different conclusion. First, that it can be countertransferentially valuable and necessary when primitive material that cannot be put into words is presented in a session. Second, by making a key demand on the analyst, it requires him to become more adept at watching out for an enactment as a black hole that revokes past experience and objects, into which the analyst may, but should not, fall. Or if he does fall, only as the sole means of understanding the "inside" of the patient and of being able to escape the gravitational pull of negativity. A more rational, distanced position does not allow the analyst to be an object to be used and to survive. In my argument, therefore, recognition of past trauma and mental states and of the survivability of the analyst as a question embodied in the analytic process need to be theorized together.

In a letter in response to the *International Journal of Psycho-Analysis*, Imre Szecsödy has written of this use of the analyst:

> I put a great emphasis on the interpersonal relationship between analysand and analyst, which can—hopefully—become a new and unique type of object relationship. Its main facets are the constancy of interest, acceptance and reliability; the systematic attempt to put the patient's welfare foremost; the suspension of

moral value-judgements and the willingness not to require that the patient conform to any particular standard of behaviour. This is providing a "holding environment" that can protect the patient from disruptive levels of unpleasure or disorganisation and can relieve the patient of a previous sense of isolation and alienation in regard to his own thoughts, wishes, and fantasies. The experience that the analyst does not retaliate, reject, move out when the patient is relating with erotic or strong negative feelings, with hostility, negativism, withdrawal, contempt—offers evidence of a unique form of acceptance.

(Szecsödy 2001, pp. 171–173)

Szecsödy is describing the possibility of a new type of object relationship, far from the dynamic of the analyst being on guard from being entrapped by the patient. His remarks also reflect the crucial reality that psychic change does not only come about through interpretation *per se*, but rather through interpretation within the context of the unconscious object relationship at a given time. This is the meaning of Winnicott's "facilitating environment" as a context for the analytic situation.

In this context, enactment takes on a different meaning and, on the part of the analyst, can be a crucial intervention. Chapter Four of this book discusses the analysis of a schizophrenic patient, but for now I will describe my destroying a clinical session by terminating it early, as at that moment I could no longer bear the massive daily cutting of the patient's body. This had continued for several weeks and, despite all my interpretative attempts, her destructive attacks on herself just increased. She cut her arms, anus, and vagina. Bandages on her arms pointed out the night's destructiveness on that part of her body, and the discomfort with which she invariably sat on the floor at the far corner of the room from myself showed the assault on her bottom. The patient's ritualized bloodletting was an element of her destructiveness that found a mutual moment of horror in my wiping her out by calling an early halt to one session. She had arrived for a Friday session with even more bandages, and wanted to commence her session as if it were utterly separate from the bodily attack. Within a couple of minutes, I "found myself" asking her to leave. She rightly confirmed that she had come at the correct time. I agreed, but said I was unable to work with her that day. She left perplexed, whilst I felt terrible, yet knowing that she had suddenly and unexpectedly approached my limit of containment. Waiting to see what the following Monday session would bring was agonizing, especially as I expected her to enact a further assault by attempting suicide over the ensuing weekend. I did nothing but stay with the aloneness of pain and the paradox that, in my opinion, the best help was to dare to leave a gap and to trust in the patient's capacity to survive my destruction of her, rather than arranging a hospital admission. I was assailed by my own demons that I was not a competent analyst and imagined I would be struck off the medical register, yet I made no attempt to contact the patient over the weekend as I thought it would primarily be self-serving.

Following the weekend, the patient arrived on time for the next session. She looked considerably better and no longer dangled bloody bandages. She began by saying that she was very grateful for what I had said and done in the previous session, as she understood it as recognition that I cared about her. Implicitly, she also meant that I was not simply allowing sessions to continue in some sort of unconscious collusion with the idea that she could just continue seriously to cut herself, as if her body did not matter. She commented that she did not know until then that I cared about her. She never cut her body again and the transference alliance was considerably strengthened. This is an example of my act of murder that enabled us to discover, in time, the traumatic early roots in severe physical and mental assaults on her.

Of course, interpretations about her state had been made in all manner of ways, always falling on stony ground. Historically, this was a repetition, as it seemed that her parents had had no concern about pain inflicted physically on her. Her response to my act was being able to begin to heal the pair of us. It was the first such recognition. The cutting ceased immediately and did not return. Such work, akin to falling into a deep dark hole and state of alarm for the analyst, is the clinical terrain of a potential for creative recovery. The patient's ability to work with me, despite such desperate destructive activities, enabled the cutting to stop. The point of being able to enter such an emotionally evocative blackness that was a recreation of her history was that now we could work together on her historical traumas, whereas in the past, and for most of her life, she was profoundly alone. Such a clinical atmosphere cannot be taught but requires a good-enough capacity to bear being in that moment and accepting one's fate—a position true for both analyst and analysand.

What I am trying to describe could therefore be understood as a deeper level of Winnicott's use of the object. By this, I mean that an act of interpretation can work by being two-sided, affecting, in differing ways, both analysand and analyst. In the presence of such primitive unconscious relationships, if the analyst remains in a clinical position of being only the observer, looking at and commenting on, then the patient realizes (often quite quickly) that the analyst is not alongside their emotional analytic journey. For those patients who have had a surfeit of destructiveness in life that has left them barely alive emotionally, the process of healing necessitates the revelation of the impact of that destructiveness both on themselves as a form of expression, and on the analyst, with each of the pair taking on the different sadistic and masochistic positions as the object is made use of.

Melanie Klein did write about the impoverished external reality for some children (1957, p. 234):

> There is no doubt that if the infant was actually exposed to very unfavourable conditions, the retrospective establishment of a good object cannot undo bad early experiences. However, the introjection of the analyst as a good object, if not based on idealization, has, to some extent, the effect of providing an internal good object where it has largely been lacking.

In this passage, Klein is quite aware of actual traumatic environmental conditions as well as a particular use of the object that can be therapeutic. However, modern Kleinians invariably leave out the impact and meaning of such real negativistic environments in their descriptions of clinical work and in theory.

For instance, a theoretical position can describe the patient as driving the analyst to be tortured as a perverse end in itself, or the idea that what is at stake is the pleasure of the destructive instinct that takes over, which then requires the analyst "to show the patient what they are doing", usually by "trapping the analyst" (Joseph 1989, p. 161). A major theoretical difference is the location of the analyst. For some analysts, the patient is doing destructive things to the analyst who, as far as possible, has to stay outside such experience in order to describe and show it to the analysand. There is a process of knowing what is going on and saying so in interpretation. Then, if the interpretation is not accepted, this, in turn, can be taken as further evidence of destructiveness and resistance towards analysis.

With the analyst outside the fray, the patient is left with various choices, depending on the scale of neurotic or psychotic defences. The more neurotic patient may now be able to see the abyss and take measures to develop ego coping mechanisms. The patients that more concern me here are those who can agree with what the analyst is saying, most likely a false self-solution based on the belief that it is psychically safer to go along with the power of the one who knows. Arguably, this is in itself an enactment, a return to a previous set of unconscious solutions, based on the belief that the grown-up knows best and certainly knows far more than anything that might conceivably arise from the analysand's own emotional-intellectual knowledge. Another possibility is that the constant stress on the analysand's destructiveness and disdain in refusing to take in the analyst's observations can lead to a fracture of the clinical frame and an early departure by the patient from treatment. It can then be regarded as a self-fulfilling prophecy, since the departure will most likely be seen as a culmination of the patient's destructiveness and a confirmation of the interpretative line that the patient is so destructive that analysis has to be destroyed. For the patient, on the other hand, departure may be understood as another escape from a domineering object, which was the very reason for seeking analysis in the first place. Such an analytic scenario could not be further removed from one based on the expectation that the analyst as object needs to be made (ill) use of, that mutual destructiveness is inevitable and even essential, and has to be experienced so that the patient may be able to understand the possibility of a new beginning and realize: "I didn't know you cared". Given the journey through destructiveness, such a moment is hardly sentimental but is the only path to a realization of a complex, often painful, authenticity.

I want to draw attention to the immense difficulties, at times, of enabling the very regressed patient to continue to attend sessions. There is a serious school of thought that suggests that such patients should be temporarily admitted to a psychiatric ward. Then either the analyst visits or the patient attends sessions brought by a nurse, or there is an analytic hiatus (Kernberg 1975, p. 188). This is an immensely complicated field since it concerns how much hatred and mental assault both analysand and analyst can bear. For the analyst, a great deal of mental and sometimes physical robustness is required. The analyst needs to be scrupulously honest with himself. For instance, it is not uncommon during psychiatric or analytic training for a patient in treatment to commit suicide. In discussions with colleagues, such events have been deeply upsetting, humiliating, and often left unresolved. The analyst in this position, with an unresolved complex about such murder, may quietly resolve to stay clear of such difficult patients and, understandably given this history, may be quick to resort to sending the patient off into "safer hands" when such terrain unexpectedly emerges.

From this perspective, hospitalization may suit the analyst best, as well as apparently suiting the patient sent away for care. However, the meaning of such sending away can be profound for the analysand, full of unconscious shards of their own sense of how impossible a burden they are. The patient may decide to ease up and once again move into a false solution to cover up the pain of the unconscious loss of the other. In such cases, it is crucial to recognize the complexity of what is being enacted, as the mental assault in the present, felt as intolerable by the analyst, may in fact have been the only operative channel for disclosing something of what was done in the past, most crucially, of who is doing what to whom. If the analyst finds they cannot bear the intensity of analytic work at this level, this should be a clarion call for consultation with a more experienced colleague as well as an occasion to think about more analysis for the analyst. In my experience, some analysts contain the unanalysed ghosts of suicided patients. I am not saying this in an accusatory way, but the insularity and narcissism of our profession, like indeed all professions, can act as a barrier, preventing colleagues from daring to put their clinical skills in order and become healed themselves. It has often been noted that borderline patients unconsciously take us to our own fault lines. Another way of putting the fundamental premise of these essays, then, is that we need as analysts to be more attuned to what these fault lines are, if we are to avoid the risk of projecting our professional anxieties onto the patient and thereby evading, or missing, the deepest, historically grounded, reality and force of their own.

* * *

Another clinically related area examined in these chapters is that of psychosomatics. As I wrote at the beginning, the ego is a body ego, and the body must therefore always be at the core of analytic work. In the psychotic experience, overwhelming trauma is dealt with in the mind, yet, for some, the mind is so overwhelmed by what it is required to contain that the body needs to "take over" some of the load. The mind needs protection from the impact of massive affect: a move from psyche to soma. The body can take over in providing the contours of associations, but these are detached from a mental capacity to free associate and emotionally feel. Thus one finds a patient who adopts particular positions on the couch—a certain rigidity of limbs or never moving—as a means of concealing earlier trauma and keeping it far distant from what threatens as some terrible knowing. Of course, there may be free associations but only up to a point, after which one can notice the inhibition in the body. This acts both to conceal and reveal. Such positional structures need to be noticed to allow for the possibility of movement away from the somatic register and towards mental curiosity. Putting into words moves psychic energy from the thing (body) presentation to word presentation that enables affect to move from an attachment to the body to that of the clinical dyad. As with the rest of an analysis, this requires time to work through the newfound memories in terms of past relationships. The patient in her psychosomatic place is alone and does not expect, nor often even wish for, the intervention of the other. The unconscious expectation is that the other is not there to help, and often (perhaps invariably in such cases) there is an historical truth to this, as the adults did not protect the infant from trauma and may even have caused it. Very often, the traumatized analysand has not had an early history of being held and cuddled by the mother, such that in adult life being touched becomes an ego-alien idea and perceived as the harbinger of further assault. This leads to the possibility that only self-holding is possible (rocking, masturbating, disturbances of feeding, etc.).

In these cases, analysis opens up a new possibility in the telling, that the listener, who may be experienced after a while as benign, can hear the patient, invariably for the first time. Noise, arising from beneath the surface of the everyday, unconsciously sought for by the analysand, may be an unexpected and new position. The patient may begin to know that the other is listening.

We return then to Ferenczi, whose view was that the traumatic (body) memory forces itself spontaneously to the fore. He describes the tic as an ego hysteria (Ferenczi 1921, p. 173), and we shall examine a case of spasmodic torticollis in Chapter Three. Ferenczi's desire was to analyse as much as possible the reasons why the mind, at times, is not able to know, conceptualize, imagine, or feel the affect. This brings Freud and Ferenczi together. For Ferenczi, penetrating deeply is to take off, tactfully, the surface cover in order to reveal Freud's "rent in the ego" (Freud 1924, p. 151) that contains descriptions of traumatic landscapes.

The chapters in this volume will seek to bear testament to life-and-death struggles lived through and survived at great expense. A domain captured by living and partly living which is uncovered by travelling through the waste lands of the mind. There is a psychic inevitability to discovering the traumatic in everyday life that reveals itself repeatedly in these chapters. What follows is an analytic journey in which the present is found as past, in the unremembered and repressed history of the patient, somewhere lost in the landscapes of the dark.

Endnote

1. Rickman can also be found in Ferenczi's paper, Child Analysis in the Analysis of Adults discussing in relation to regression: "whether I kept remedies at hand in order to intervene if necessary to save a patients life. I was able to reply that I did, but that, so far, had never had to use them" (Ferenczi, 1931, p. 138).

CHAPTER TWO

Formulation of interpretations in clinical practice

Lear: Who is it that can tell me who I am.
Fool: Lear's Shadow.

—William Shakespeare, *King Lear*

Analysis is an interaction between two people. The patient brings his own highly individual difficulties and sufferings to the analyses, which are the affects and intellectual thoughts referring to his unconscious object relationships. The analyst brings what he hopes is a sound and adequate technique, which also must be highly individual. We know this from the diversity of points from which an analyst can set off in one of several directions, especially if we can agree no single way is correct on the analytic journey. The analyst has to make an interpretation in such a way as to lower the patient's resistance, through an understanding of the conflict in the patient's mind. Yet this seemingly simple idea can be undertaken in different ways.

A great deal of the analytic work is expected, by both parties, to be accomplished in words—the patient telling his story through free association and the analyst speaking heris interpretation to make the unconscious conscious. What the patient cannot say, he brings by way of enactment, in what he does during his life in analysis, in the analytic hour, as well as the enactment of the dream in the session. Congruently, the analyst also brings to the session much that is not said, but can be thought of as a particularity called "the holding environment".

The patient enters the room, which is the working analytic environment. Already the body has entered into another space, through a door. Depending on the unconscious associations of an individual analysand, this beginning can develop fantasies, already nascent, from the fear of entering mother's body to entering the secret garden and more. The room has a certain level of lighting and ambient temperature, neither too harsh nor extreme. It has a particular couch: for some, it is narrow; for others, wide; it can be leather or carpeted. For some, it provides associations towards bed and bedtime; for others, sex or being looked after. Cushions may have replaceable paper covers, or the same cushions can hold the smell of previous patients. Each of these small movements is part of the symphony of the analytic environment in which a particular patient finds him or herself, and this may be acceptable or not for the patient, according to his own history. Does the analyst stand at the start and end of the session? Is there physical contact with handshaking? Does the session end with ritual words? All such matters point to the idiosyncrasies of the analyst within his culture and aren-ever neutral propositions.

The footnote in Freud's *Two Principles of Mental Functioning* has been pointed out by many before, including Winnicott, but it is worth reiterating here:

> It would rightly be objected that an organization which was a slave to the pleasure principle and neglected the reality of the external world could not maintain itself with the shortest time, so that it could not have come into existence at all. The employment of a fiction like this is however justified when one considers that the infant—provided that one includes with it the care he receives from his mother—does almost realize the psychical system of this kind.
>
> (Freud 1911, p. 220)

The patient has difficulty in perceiving reality. The analytic environment is perceived as a peculiar psychic system, and the patient has a view, real and imaginary, of the care he received in the past and receives in the present. Winnicott, recognizing that Freud is paying "full tribute to the function of maternal care" (Winnicott 1960, p. 39) and using the concept of the holding environment, expects that its specific conditions—of original maternal care—will appear, at some time and in some form, in the transference. How the analyst holds the patient, in the working environment of the consulting room, as well as his particular character, is part of the clinical dyad, and will be observable at times to the analysand.

Strachey (1934) makes it very plain that the requirement of the interpretation is to provide small doses of reality to the patient, such that in time their misperceptions of projections onto the analyst can be seen in a real light. Here, "reality" may refer to the reality of the patient's internal relationships. However, that very concept of reality must also include the reality of the real things that the analyst contributes to the environment of the analysis. One can think that the analytic environment, and by this I mean the colour of the walls, ornamentation, feel of the couch cover, temperature, noise levels, and so on, are all designed to allow for the possibility of the patient feeling safe enough to move towards regression. It is not uncommon that various pieces of unwanted transferences from the analyst's own analysis creep in to his practice. For instance, the way the analyst organizes his practice is often highly modelled on his perception of the way his own analyst did things. Already one may be unconsciously providing for the perceptive enough patient, a dual model of oneself as analyst but also one's own analyst inside oneself. Such things are not necessarily adverse unless of course they exist in an unknown state to the analyst and as such can provide unthoughtful enactments that can become an impingement on the patient.

Content and context

One listens to the patient's associations, always trying to balance the *content* and the *context*. When I have an understanding of one, I place it next to my understanding of the other, to deduce if they match so as to obtain corroboration that my understanding may be in a right direction. If there is any discord then I have to wonder why and not be taken in too quickly with "understanding". An example would be a patient who is giving plenty of Oedipal material about a relationship to the analyst as father—a rich and understandable content, yet speaking in a flat, unemotional atmosphere, as if one is supposed to be simply excited more with the knowledge of the content. There is something missing beneath the superficial knowingness and the useful internal question would be: why am I supposed to be roused by understanding this material, who am I being in the transference, what are the expectations of me? Perhaps the flat affect is itself indicating something which is a truer recognition of the mood state of the child projected into the analyst. The patient can unconsciously enact being the exciting parent, quite separate from the mood of the child which is perceived by the analyst. The excitement and the flattened affect together become a cipher for a double mood state that invariably the child had difficulty understanding in their relationship with a parent, being unable to process their own affect. Some parents unconsciously (mis)use children as a dump for their own surfeit of emotionality. The adult, rather than process or contain their own unconscious emotional life, can split off a dose of affect into their child.

An important and often difficult aspect of this work of counter-transference is the analyst's natural and at times profoundly ambivalent response to having to take in such experience, which can at times be almost impossible to bear. It allows us to question how the child is expected to contain that which we grown-ups find so very difficult to understand and process. The analyst is required to have discovered from his own analysis and life experience resilience to the unbearable. It is part of the two-step process to be able to be in the shoes of the patient and then return to oneself, in order to process the material. Such projections are well beyond an intellectual process, being connected to powerful affects. At times, the projections into the analyst have a suddenness and intensity well beyond just stepping into the patient's position or mind. It can stir up either or both in the dyad and is very valuable for being able to so do. Yet it requires of the analyst a capacity to ride a rollercoaster of emotions.

Analysts, at times, can tend to get caught up in a particular way of thinking, which may imply they are not thinking. Bion writes in relation to -K:

> Some patients who are concerned to prove their superiority to the analyst by defeating his attempts at interpretation can be shown that they are mis-understanding the interpretations to demonstrate that an ability to mis-understand is superior an ability to understand.

> (Bion 1962, p. 95)

This equally applies to the analyst, for example with the persistent interpretation of weekend or separation anxiety (too readily offered and understood) which might be a cover for a deeper pattern of the analyst's existence or non-existence in the sessions. The implication is that an analyst is more comfortable in his own theoretical order rather than waiting to see where the patient may roam in a session. If the analyst wears his theory in a too-present manner, it is searched for in the associations of the patient, as if it is the most relevant matter at that moment. To turn Bion's idea around it is as if the analyst is concerned to prove his superiority to the patient. Patients who have been brought up in the domain of such superior adults will quickly know the atmosphere. The thinking analyst may stumble into such territory and then realize countertransferentially that they are playing an unconscious superior role in the early life of their patient and can learn from it. Such understanding may lead to a different kind of interpretation about the meanings of, say, being superior and inferior in the life and relationships of the patient. The curious patient and analyst will then desire to know more of the origins of such formations.

Analysts can become embroiled in an unconscious defence reaction to the pain of the other. Rosenfeld, writing cogently of the early hopes that a detailed "interpretation of envy" would prevent impasse in the treatment, also developed the theme of the problem of the analyst's superiority. He wrote:

> It is inevitable that envy arises in human development and that the child, or the patient in analysis, is going to feel small or inferior at some times. I particularly have in mind situations when the child, or patient, feels put down and may actually have been put down by the parents or by other children, or in analysis, by the analyst. In my experience, it is when a patient feels accepted and helped in analysis and feels that he/she has some space to think and grow, that envy gradually diminishes. For these reasons, interpretations of envy should not be repeated too often … . An over-emphasis on the interpretation of envy, or the over-valuing of the analyst's contributions as compared to that of the patient is a frequent cause of impasse.

> (Rosenfeld 1987, p. 266)

Yet such an impasse, if found and recognized, can be explored as an enactment of early history both real and imaginary, perceivable by the patient as a thing performed precisely because it cannot be put into speech.

However tactful and respectful one is towards the patient, the given interpretation can be experienced as a thing rather than a word which wounds as it penetrates. The original meaning of the Greek word *poema* (poem) means not just an utterance but also a "thing made". Certainly, for some patients, penetration by the analyst's words is sexualized and experienced as a phallic intrusion by the analyst into their ear. One may interpret in a quietly modulated voice in order to create a safe tone or atmosphere. The development of the atmosphere of analysis—the creation of the space for thought prior to words—needs its own time to evolve. In a similar way to the emergence of unconscious affect through sound patterns in music (say a Beethoven symphony in all its polyphonic complexities), the ebb and flow and pitch and rhythm conveys the emotional load from unconscious to unconscious. It is pertinent to ask why it can be so difficult for the analyst to give a transference interpretation. How can it be so difficult if it is what one has been trained to do? Far from being an obstacle to treatment, a failure of the analytic process, such as a moment of hesitancy, may be a crucial act for the analyst, who at that moment is exposed to the danger of the patient's Id being directed at him without ambiguity, that is, with an unmodified affect of love and hate.

To use a metaphor, how does one approach the Minotaur to kill the symptoms gripping the patient alone in the subterranean labyrinth? If one rushes in, this leads inevitably to grief and death. Yet the unconscious anxiety of the analyst can often lead to a compelling desire to say something, as if the analyst's speech maintains his aliveness in the face of an immensely difficult moment. Whilst such a scenario might help the analyst, it is unlikely to be in the realms of the needs of the patient. The moment then has to be inspired, and what of inspiration or intuition? The analyst has internalized a particular view of psychoanalysis, has a particular analytic experience himself, has his own analytic "gifts", and has his own particular theoretical position which can compel him to leap into a moment of creativity with his patient. Winnicott wrote, "A patient said to me: 'Good management (ego care) such as I have experienced during this hour is a feed' (id-satisfaction)" (Winnicott 1960, p. 141). However, such creative moments might be hard to cultivate.

No two analysts are alike. As Balint remarked:

> It is remarkable that the advocates of different methods of interpretation as well as their critics are inclined to think that only their

technique is correct, and consider all other methods bad, or even harmful. This arouses a suspicion that some personal element may be playing a part in the evolution of the various ways of solving the problem, since differences and effectiveness do not correspond to the stress made upon them.

(A. Balint & M. Balint 1939, p. 226)

Thus, there can be difficulty in the scientific exchange between differently held theoretical views and their incumbent emotional attachments. Furthermore, each analysis with a different patient interacting with the analyst is unique from every other analysis. To my mind, this is not about inducting the patient into one's own theoretical *mélange* of analytic thought. More importantly, it is to establish a *unique* dialogue in a language between analyst and analysand which may even be beyond theory. Theories are of a generalized nature and it is profoundly difficult to think of a theory of individual style. Sandler has written cogently in this area between psychoanalytic concepts and psychoanalytic practice (Sandler 1985).

One needs to interpret material in a balanced unconscious position with the "here and now" of the present, the transference and in time, when more is known, an understanding back to the past. To rush to the past may indicate that the heat of the present affect between patient and analyst is being avoided. However, the transference in the here and now and, in particular, present affect which might or can be a repetition of the past (as expressed by *après coup*) must be kept in the mind of the analyst. Such movement can be overwhelming and even, at times, beyond interpretation. Certainly, the dialectic of tension between past and present history and here and now can be very difficult to discern and untangle. The drama of enactment that the patient brings in the session can be very powerful when it is in the idiom beyond words. One must always estimate individually the tendency to flee from the present and the power of attraction of the past as a balance to be discovered within the analytic encounter. With trauma belonging to the past and the disposition to trauma belonging to the present, the character of the transference will consist of movement between these two positions. We see this process perhaps most clearly in psychosis, where Freud wrote of the patch covering the rent in the mind (Freud 1924, p. 151) acting as a cover and also as a reconstruction. Every interpretation is a reconstruction when it is in the area of psychotic working, as Juliet

Mitchell has suggested (private communication). If one puts into words the wordless psychotic experience, this can only happen after a period of time when the analyst has recovered from the impact of the wordless projective identification. If one interprets the experience of what the patient has attempted to do to the analyst now or some months later, it is already a reconstruction.

After attending a few sessions, a new patient, in spite of much urgency, just stopped coming to sessions. She asked to return after six weeks, having sought out, in the meantime, her old therapist from many years ago. She was pleased with the initial contact with him until she gradually realized he was too old, being in his eighties. She returned, and during that next session she decided that there had been something superficial about her previous work. We deduced that her therapist had signified her father who, when she was about twenty, had rescued her from very difficult circumstances. Yet she had not thought that the act of leaving my practice without warning mattered. She had an opinion that it had no feeling in it for herself and that I should also have been unconcerned. This was another level of construction in which she lived a life expecting very little of others. She had a flamboyant red polka-dotted handkerchief in her hand for much of the session, wiping her nose and waving it around. It seemed a colourful flag in the midst of a sea of grey. It seemed to represent for me an idea that people should not, or could not, or even did not mind, what was happening. The session ended and the patient left. On leaving my consulting room, I found that she had unconsciously managed to trap her handkerchief between the two doors of the consulting room, with a little corner exposed in order to be seen. She was unconsciously signalling that she wanted to leave something of herself behind, that she had a reluctance to leave, or that she would need a surface reason to return in order to collect it. Yet in addition to those possibilities, I was struck by the notion that something was trapped, even pinched, between two doors. Perhaps it was an enactment constructing a moment, which, if it had been her finger, would have been most painful; yet it was also a painless nothing. Thus the moment offered an analytic direction to explore further about how throughout her life painful things were minimized and flamboyantly waved away. Perhaps the two doors trapping the red cloth were an unconscious representation of her parents, catching her in between themselves as represented by her becoming caught between two analysts recently. Such a beginning provided plenty of interesting thoughts to consider, especially connecting to her wish to depart from treatment, because in staying, painful affect from her past would need to be felt and expressed—something she had resisted all her life. This is an example of how reconstruction of past affect can contribute to developing an atmosphere of therapeutic benefit.

One of the hardest parts of clinical work may be in "bearing not knowing". In order to attempt to reduce the tension of not knowing, particularly during a long silent period, the analyst may be tempted to organize the patient, to make sense of the patient's complaints and illness, and to start to say something and "interpret". This may temporarily be easier for the analyst; it may superficially be gratifying for the patient, but remains well away from deeper strands of unconscious phantasy life. It may well be that the most appropriate intervention at a particular moment or session, or even a series of sessions, is to continue with a holding silence. This can be very hard to do, but it can be an essential tool if the alternative is a false analytical rhetoric.

Silence comes in many forms. It is often the case that the early life of the patient has been full of events, words, activity, and noise. The idea of a period of quietness may not be a signal of resistance. Rather, it can be a newly found possibility of being with another person in silence, either thinking thoughts or, for a time, being empty as a prelude to further work together. For this, the analyst must be able to be comfortable enough in such terrain. The analyst needs to be able to bear silence and not rush to fill the space. Of course, a different type of silence can be defensive or aggressive. As well as waiting to see what emerges, if it continues for many sessions, it can become the predominant theme, which may need to be noticed and interpreted as resistance. However, saying this is rather unhelpful, better to add to the interpretation an idea about why. The analyst can think about what might be being repeated, such as who did not talk to whom in the earlier life of the child. An enactment in silence may have a profound content which begs the question "who is doing what to whom and why?". In such happenings, the analyst is not only a receiver of silence from the patient but is also a participant in the experience in the session.

A patient, who in analysis had realized the emotional impact of having been a victim of incest by her father, spent a session berating me for not being seduced by her. She was able to realize herself that she had to disavow a particular phantasy that, if not now, I would succumb to her charms at some time in the future. The realization that I would not sexually invade her or let her invade me had a great impact on her. The next session she was totally silent, as I was also. At the end of the session, she stood up and with an authentic gratitude, thanked me for bearing the silence with her. If I had said anything that session, it would have been actively intruding into her space, enacting in analysis her father's physical invasion of her body. Instead, she knew she was in a relationship in which a boundary was fully respected at an appropriate time.

When we train as psychoanalysts, we inevitably pick up and develop our own internal language of what analysis is about. We find comfort in certain formulations of unconscious process, and it is possible that our like and dislike of certain theoretical models is also a reflection of the importance of our own early object relationships. Being surrounded by a particular theoretical formulation can act as a protection from the impingement of the patient's conscious and unconscious effects on the analyst. At this point, we can ask whether the analyst needs such protection; or what price is paid for protecting oneself from the patient in such a way. Such a perspective leads to the examination of the actual language the analyst and the patient use with each other. Often, they can both use words as if there is a commonality of meaning, which is just not present in the session. The patient may often use a noun as if helpfully to describe something. Yet we know from Freud's discovery of displacement and condensation that we may be offered some words and phrases that are only surface phenomena. It may be a critical factor not to swallow an understanding of a word until the analyst is quite sure of many of the meanings and particularities of usage.

Some analysts have developed the technique of speaking back particular words to the patient from the patient's already spoken language. This, I think, holds dangers. It supposes that the word has a common understanding between the two. It is likely that resistance is concealed in this way and a pseudo-understanding can be the result. It is as if in apparently finding the link word, then the analyst is speaking the patient's language. Beneath the surface of such discourse, miscommunication may be a dominant perspective, and in turn it can develop into an unconscious enactment of false understanding, which can have its roots in early object relations full of the affect of lost moments of connectedness. The analysand may be unconsciously taking the part of a parent, not connecting with the analyst who is in the role of the analysand feeling perplexed, misunderstood, and even alone in the discourse. More useful is the analyst's capacity to put the word back to the patient, with a particular tonality, as if the word is said in inverted commas, as a thing given, but as yet not totally unwrapped and revealed.

Of course, the patient may have a similar problem with the analyst's language—which ought to be free of jargon. This can be difficult because we are so used to discussing and talking our technical language at supervision, seminars, and conferences, as if it is the language of clinical work. At its worst, the patient begins to pick up a fragment of the new psychobabble—the patient learns the analyst's language. Here, I think, something has become misdirected—it is like the child fitting in with the adult's speech and way of doing things, and it may occur more in those with early deprivational damage—where learning to fit in and to adapt chameleon-like is the best way of surviving future attacks.

Looking more specifically at the use of sounds in language, there is the modulation of voice, pitch, and rhythm to consider. The patient can certainly notice such musicality, looking for the inner feelings beyond the words of the analyst towards them, of possible favour or hatred. It is here that the analyst needs great control, needing to speak in an ordinarily modulated way, but also inwardly having a grasp of the intensity of the affect that he might have desired to add to his interpretative sentence if it had not been for the close gaze of his own ego that prevents such self-disclosure through an unconscious eruption of words.

Such countertransference affect is of great interest. The vital point of interaction between patient and analyst is in the word, and it is at this place that the libidinal relationship of the analyst with his patient may escape, because language exists to be a framework for the discharge of highly charged affect. I am reminded of how Paula Heimann used to insist that one talks to the patient by using the pronoun "we". She saw this as an essential part of the process of binding the patient to the analyst as part of the construction of the treatment alliance. The use of the pronoun "you" in an interpretation can push the analysand directly against the working alliance, and essentially it is unconsciously understood as the analyst driving the patient away. This would be poignantly so for those patients who had experienced parental neglect, such that there was an unconscious, or even conscious, expectation that they would be pushed away again. Even when the analysand recognizes the clinical "we", it often needs to be attacked to ascertain whether it is real and viable or about a surface posture by the analyst. At the same time, of course, we have to be careful with that "we" not to assume a pseudo-togetherness or unconscious complicity on the part of the patient.

The clinical atmosphere can be thought of as a creative potential space for the possibility of the patient imbibing the interpretation. It is a partnership between two people. These two people are not equal. They have different functions that are complementary. The analyst who adopts a superior position, as the one with knowledge, is skewing the transference, or enacting it. Analytic work can be done together by the analyst–patient dyad or by the patient alone in the presence of the other. At another level, this can also represent the vital importance of the patient having to face the nature of difference, between "me" and other, which includes the psychic representation of masculinity and femininity. Qualities of masculinity and femininity, or active and passive, are unconsciously attached from early history to the role of mother and the role of father (without assuming which is active). The interactions between the parents around power, tenderness, love and hate, and sado-masochism become introjected in the child and become aspects of character to be identified or disidentified with. Such identificates, full of affect, can be projected into the analyst and interacted with unconsciously.

These questions can have profound consequences for analytic treatment. In his paper "Confusion of Tongues", Ferenczi drew attention to the countertransference feelings that are a re-creation of the original trauma in object relationships, which can be the pointer to the interpretative line. The analyst is inevitably put in the unconscious position of being part of the early object relationship system, usually the parent in relation to the patient-child, or the other way round, carrying the child's affect in relation to the patient being the adult. Over fifty years ago, Ferenczi warned:

> If we keep up our cool, educational attitude […] we tear to shreds the last thread that connects him to us. The patient gone off into his trance *is a child indeed*, who no longer reacts to intellectual explanations only perhaps to maternal friendliness; without it he feels lonely and abandoned in his greatest need, i.e., in the same unbearable situation which at one time led to the splitting of his mind and eventually to his illness; thus it is no wonder that the patient cannot but repeat now the symptom formation exactly as he did at the time when his illness started.
>
> (Ferenczi 1933, p. 160)

What is spoken, together with the affect imbued in one's interpretation, is the essential feature. Real affect in the interpretation is often what actually reaches down to touch the split parts of the patient and the intellect of the sentence then has a chance to bring the split together. Interpretation involving affect can bring together a split between mind and body.

From time to time, a patient may impose onto the interpretation their own superego affect and hear the interpretation in quite a harsh mode. When the analyst has enough evidence that this is located in the patient, rather than the patient perceiving some of the latent affect of the analyst towards him, she can make a further interpretation, for instance about the use the patient makes of the interpretation and, in particular, the way the patient's superego has heard the analyst's words. The patient may well be unable to take in good analytic food until his defensive organization that his perception that all interpretations are harmful is faced. One can now make the statement that there is no such thing as an interpretation, only an interpretation that includes its aftermath, that is, how it is used by the patient, which is akin to the contribution that the baby makes towards the meal of the milk from the breast. Analyst–analysand, mother environment–baby, both dyadic sets and pairs work together to be partners in the unfolding work. The whole of an interpretation includes insight, affect, experience, and the aftermath of its having been made.

Clinical material

I now want to discuss a particular few moments from a clinical session of a patient in analysis, which cannot contain nor describe all the different possibilities of discourse that have been discussed up to now. Perhaps the most truthful discourse of a particular fragment of analysis is silence. As soon as it becomes material to be offered through a transformation, beyond the consulting room, such as in writing, its beginning, causalities, character, development, past, and future are altered to some degree or another. Yet what else is to be done other than to press on with the task?

This is a fragment of work with a middle-aged woman in analysis who came from a background in which father was away at war when she was a little girl and mother was formal and distant. Servants used to run the family life, until wartime privation caused this environmental holding to cease. Mother, "unable to cook an egg", took to her bed, with the expectation that her daughter would manage to look after both herself and mother. Over some years, I had heard about this period of childhood on several occasions, always told with a sense of distance and with only a token amount of affect from the patient. In particular, there was a recurring memory of mother being continually in bed upstairs, and when the daughter returned from school, the daughter would go into the downstairs lounge—mother and daughter occupying two different spaces and even two different floors in the house.

Despite functioning at a high intellectual level, this particular woman was perplexed by her peculiar symptom of not being able to look at me or "my side" of the consulting room. The first session after a Christmas break found the patient rushing into the consulting room, lying down, and saying that she had (experienced) a lot of dreams and could remember two fragments. In the first, she was on a large cruise liner. On board were all her relatives and friends. She fell overboard and the ship steamed on. A small boat was nearby and tried several times to help her. She was dismissive of this and instead attempted to swim after the liner. In the second dream, recounted immediately following the first, the patient was coming to her analytic session. When she arrived at the front door of the consulting room, she was surprised to discover that the door had a porch added in front of it. She was carrying a tool wrapped up. She thought that the tool was a harrow (a rake) and she left it by the porch before entering. The patient then stopped, and there was an uncomfortable silence for some twelve minutes. It seemed appropriate not to intervene but to allow the silence its space to be in the session.

Eventually, the patient went on to say something of the difficult atmosphere at Christmas, especially in relation to her daughter, who tried to needle her by saying "you hate me, don't you?". Her daughter often said this, the mother would decline to answer, and her daughter continued to remonstrate. It seemed that we were in the realm of speech, of what can, must, and must not be said and how. After a pause, I said that I found it difficult to understand how her saying she was not going to answer the question would quieten her daughter, as it still left her daughter to think that her mother thought that she did hate her (and, of course, if the situation of nagging continued, the daughter's wish would come true). At once, the patient responded by agreeing, saying that she had made various pertinent comments over the years which had helped much more cogently. Then I made an interpretation that what she had just said was like the second dream in which she has a tool but this is left outside the consulting room. An aspect of the patient that can function and think is left and a gap ensues in her thinking. The patient agreed. She then talked about her difficult feeling of hatred, as if it was sticking out of herself. I interpreted that this "hatred sticking out" may be similar to something sticking out of my door—a porch in her dream. She now could vocalize something of her hatred of me—initially quite a furious attack on my silence after she had spoken. She had felt in my silence that I had not been listening to her or had been ignoring her. The patient felt that at least I should have told her that I had heard what she said when she came in the room. I interpreted that I had noticed that there had been an uncomfortable silence after she had rushed to tell me the dreams, and that it was this silence that had been intolerable. I had no way of making a dream interpretation as I was waiting for her to tell me the context of her Christmas break; what it had been like and, once she had supplied something of its atmosphere, then her dream might have been understood. She said she knew this, and yet she was still angry with me despite realizing that I was only trying to do analysis. What was at stake, therefore, as well as the detail of individual interpretations, was something we might call its scale. After a short while, I interpreted that it was as if she was waiting for me to make a large boat interpretation—that she was only interested in that. Any notion of a small boat helping her was not felt by her to be of much use, perhaps in the same way as she left the tool outside and then, in the dream, she is left alone to drown. She thought this was true. She did expect me to say something large and complete, and could see analysis was really only in small parts of understanding, yet she still had an overwhelming sense of my not being connected with her and a sense of anger at my non-responsiveness in the silence.

Now I could make the "deeper" interpretation that in the silence she perceived me as the distant mother who is upstairs, in a different room from her, uncaring of her state of being, and also I am a distant father who is missing from her concurrently. I also linked it to the transference, in that she also perceives me as the big boat steaming away from her during the break and her not thinking much of her own small-boat capacity for thinking and looking after herself with her own mind in my absence. She agreed with some enthusiasm and the session ended. What mattered was her capacity for thought. But no less crucially, while this contained an unmistakable reference to the present of the analysis, what was also struggling to emerge—through the silent hesitations—was an allusion to the past, to the history that had so heightened the question of silence, becoming meaningful interpretation, with such significance.

I want now to look at some of my thoughts during the session. I was confronted with a rush of dream material after a break, without further elaboration, as if analysis should just continue, without any concern about a gap in treatment. In the very uncomfortable silence, I realized I knew nothing about what she and her object relationships had got up to in my absence over Christmas. This was the point of intense resistance. Without such a context of the session, any interpretive work on the dreams would be theoretical and symbolic and, I thought, would be pseudo-analysis. In my countertransference, I was left feeling perplexed that I had thoughts about her mental life, but in the absence of knowing what was going on beyond the patient's inner world. I think that I was invited to be the little girl in the downstairs room, who had a keen intellect, back from school, knowing something was the matter. Yet, upstairs, in another compartment, mother existed in a different and separate world. It was only by connecting context and content that an analytic thought could be created.

I thought that to rush to interpret an aspect of her dream of me sailing away from her, as a description of her feeling left during the recent break from treatment, might be accepted logically but without it being connected to a deeper affect. Here it made sense of the daughter/mother interaction in which discussion and feelings seem to be vague and out of context and perplexing, although someone hated someone else and it was "harrowing". We come upon an example of a particular word as a word object, which both smoothes over the surface and at the same time contains an affective meaning of emotional distress. The word itself carries the dissonance of making something tidy and at the same time evokes pain in digging beneath the surface. In this matrix, there is a sense of her feeling hated by her mother and also by me in the transference. The point of maximum affect in the session is not the dreams but the silent aftermath, which allows an unconscious enactment that is proceeding to become conscious in time.

In this, I was the silent analyst, waiting and thinking and not rushing to say something just in order to break the silent tension and make the patient or myself necessarily feel better. In time, the patient was able to extract an element of affect towards me (and unconsciously perceived from me) called hate, about her perception of my silent treatment of her. It could be perceived in the material of the porch that stuck out. One can examine all this material in terms of the difference between the sexes, big and little boats—parts of my room that stick out (the porch) and her "tool" which she leaves behind. At different levels, it's her latent phallic state—a desire that it would be preferable to be like father away from her ill mother; beyond this is her anxiety of being in the vicinity of the mother, unconsciously perceived as phallic—the ineffable, unapproachable genital that is the mother, transferentially located in the area of the room which I inhabit. It must not be gazed upon as it is expected to be a dangerous sight, like the medusa's head turning all who gaze on her to stone. Here, we are back at her profound and primitive psychotic anxiety, with her inability to look at half of my room, containing the analytic tool. For the patient to find creativity in the analysis, the identification of the analyst as the dangerous phallic mother needs to move towards discovering the use of the analytic relationship as creative and the interpretation, as imbued with concern, rather than as a harrowing tool to fear.

From the point of view of reconstruction, what also clearly emerges is of the utmost use to have some knowledge of the early life history of the patient. My knowledge of a repeated fragment of this, in terms of a mother distanced upstairs, an absent father, and a daughter apparently doing all the looking after, is then of critical value not just as an interesting thought about the past, but as a way of locating the transference in the present. A buried affect from the past can then be brought together with the enactment in the session between the patient and the analyst.

If the X mas break was crucial, it was not therefore only in the here and now but as part of a key evocation of the past. The work in this session highlights the use of content and context as a way of focusing the material. It also shows how pseudo-analysis is invited in an intellectual way rather than allowing the possibility of locating the affect in the present tense of the session. What matters, therefore, are the connections between the present transference and the reconstruction of the past, in particular how the material relating to a break in treatment arises from a deep rather than a surface position. What we are then able to see is the Oedipal and pre-Oedipal theoretical structures emerge as part of the thinking process of the analyst to be worked through later in the analysis.

In the knowledge that in this vignette I have left aside a huge amount of analytic work already done, I have highlighted specific countertransference material that gave direction to the analytic stance. To quote Baranger, Baranger, and Mom:

> we cannot function with a concept of definitive history. It is well known that the analysand comes with one history (sometimes quite remarkably poor) and "ends" with a different history with much subtler figures, moments of happiness and unhappiness, parents who are "good" and "bad" depending on moments and situations. The history we are left with can never be considered as an absolute term, as the "truth" substituted for the lie.
>
> (Baranger, Baranger & Mom 1988, p. 125)

It is also worth remembering, at this moment, the opening sentence of Tolstoy's *Anna Karenina*: "All happy families resemble one another, each unhappy family is unhappy in its own way" (Tolstoy 1877, p. 1).

"I may remind you", Ferenczi wrote,

> that patients do not react at theatrical phrases but only to real sincere sympathy. Whether they recognise the truth by the intonation or color of our voice, or by the words we use, or in some other way, I cannot tell. In any case, they share a remarkable, almost clairvoyant knowledge about the thoughts and emotions that go on in the analyst's mind. To deceive a patient in this respect seems to be hardly possible and if one tries to do so it leads only to bad consequences.
>
> (Ferenczi 1933, p. 161)

Here, Ferenczi is again drawing attention to the necessity for the analyst to be in his own authenticity and state of reality as a character. The analytic pair meets each other with their own unconscious character, symbols, and myths. Gaugin believed that action was required to search out for the symbolic, as a way or directing and expanding life towards what he considered was the larger forces of the mythic. Whereas Van Gogh thought that myth sprang from the very mundane variations of the ordinary found in life (Artaud 1947). If the ordinary, for some analysands consists of having been and still expecting to be in experiences of trauma, then such fragments can become metaphorically shards of a broken mosaic, which are far from ordinary life. (Artaud 1947) These ordinary things in life, especially small pieces of flitting thoughts, need to be regarded as the necessary engine for discovery. The question again appears about whether one steps in to the fray, interpretation at the ready or by steady notice and apperception of the field of vision one delicately tries not disturb, holding off interfering (with the interpretation), allowing the discovery to make itself known, by the analysand reaching it themselves. The analyst can create a particular analytic atmosphere for the analysand's self discovery rather than being told. This is very different from the inevitable experiential knowledge that the analyst has at his disposal that can lead to a conventional interpretation. The expectation of an Oedipal interpretation, for instance, is very different from the falsification of such expectation, in which the next series of thoughts and words spoken cause disturbance. I am deliberately not discriminating analyst from analysand from such moments as the direction of the next association, coming from the unexpected unconscious, can and, at times, must confound both. Such would be a point of maximum emergence of lost affect. As Kermode points out, in writing about literature (2000, p. 18), the more certainly we shall feel that the fiction under consideration is one of those which, by upsetting the ordinary balance of our naïve expectations, is finding something out for us, something real. The falsification of an expectation can be terrible, as in the death of Cordelia (*King Lear*); it is a way of finding something out that we should, on our more conventional way to the end, have closed our eyes to. Obviously, it would not work if there were not a certain rigidity in the set of our expectations.

And what is analysis other than stories, fixed narratives given to us by the grown-ups as well as understandings we have arrived at to "explain" the phenomena of our family life; what Freud called "family romance" (Freud 1909). Discovering more about the real in our lives is disturbing. If we cannot break free of them, we have to understand them. Paradoxically, further understanding may emerge after breaking free.

Such an analytic journey is not a direct one, but such movements that I have been developing are examples of the method of analysis in a session—to open up the space for the development of free association. On this journey, we have passed the terrains of the interpretative environment, the problems of theories, the use of language, silence, reconstruction, and countertransference. One has to approach the making of an interpretation each time as being a new interpretation because the patient will certainly perceive the affect that one brings to an interpretation that is hackneyed and theoretical or even from a manual. The point of making the unconscious conscious with a fullness of associated affect may also be a moment of reconnection with unconscious truth for the analyst as well as the patient.

I will end this chapter with a quote from a letter to a friend of Rilke about writing poetry.

> Always at the commencement of work, that first innocence must be re-achieved, you must return to that unsophisticated spot where the angel discovered you when he brought you the first binding message. If the angel deigns to come, it would be because you have convinced him, not with tears, but with your humble resolve to be always beginning: to be a beginner!
>
> (Rilke, November 1920)

CHAPTER THREE

Hysteria and mourning—a psychosomatic case

Of course missing a mistress and the jealousy that lingers on afterwards are physical illnesses just as much as tuberculosis or leukaemia. Yet we need to distinguish among the physical maladies between those that are caused by a purely physical agency and those that act on the body only through the media of the intellect. Above all, if part of our intellect that serves as a medium of transmission is memory—that is if the cause is annulled or removed—however cruel our suffering is, however deep seems the disturbance wrought on our organism, it is extremely rare, given the power of thought to renew itself or rather its inability to remain unchanged, unlike bodily tissues, for the prognosis to be unfavourable.

—Marcel Proust, *The Fugitive* (1925, p. 608)

In *Studies on Hysteria*, Freud and Breuer write about tracing "the most various symptoms which are ostensibly spontaneous and as one might say, idiopathic products of hysteria are just as strictly related to the precipitating trauma" (Breuer & Freud 1893–1895, p. 4). They go on to describe various illnesses, including disorders in the nature of tic. There have, however, been very few case reports in the recent literature on the treatment of such cases.

Modern analytic literature often stresses the need to recognize psychobiological bedrock. I argue that an analyst can too quickly accept such a diagnosis as a way of covering over the traumatic gap. Freud, in his paper *Neurosis and Psychosis*, writes in relation to the genesis of delusions:

> a fair number of analyses have taught us that the delusion is found applied like a patch over the place where originally a rent had appeared in the ego's relation to the external world. If this pre-condition of a conflict with the external world is not much more noticeable to us than it now is, that is because, in the clinical picture of the psychosis, the manifestations of the pathogenic process are often overplayed by manifestations of an attempt at cure or, a reconstruction.
>
> (Freud 1924, p. 151)

Freud goes on to assert that the aetiology common to the onset of a psychoneurosis and of the psychosis always remain the same: "It consists in a frustration, a non fulfilment, of one of those childhood wishes which are forever undefeated and which are so rooted in our phylogenetically determined organisation" (ibid., p. 151). This is a statement about the importance of unconscious fantasy life rather than aspects of reality.

Ferenczi was particularly interested in finding the balance between fantasy and trauma. He writes in a letter to Freud:

> In all cases in which I have penetrated deeply enough, I found the traumatic-hysterical basis for the illness ... . The critical view that gradually formed in me in the process was that psychoanalysis engages too much one-sidedly in obsessional neurosis and character analysis i.e., ego psychology, neglecting the organic hysterical basis for the analysis; the cause lies in the over estimation of fantasy and the under estimation of traumatic reality in pathogenesis.
>
> (Ferenczi & Freud 1920–1933, p. 376)

Here is a statement that points in the direction of the need to play with such balances during the course of the analysis.

Ferenczi's view was that the traumatic (body) memory forces itself spontaneously to the fore. He describes the tic as an ego hysteria

(Ferenczi 1921, p. 173). Ferenczi's desire was to analyse as much as possible the reasons that the mind, at times, is not able to know, conceptualize, imagine, or feel the affect such that the body is required to take over and carry, as it were, the unconscious emotional load. His idea of penetrating deeply is to tactfully take off the surface cover in order to reveal the "rent in the ego" that for Ferenczi contains descriptions of traumatic landscapes.

This chapter describes the impact of re-finding the lost affect in the disappearance of the patient's mother when the patient was two years old. The feelings generated then and subsequently in unconscious phantasy life became, in Bollas's term, the idiom of his life (Bollas 1992). It was only after the development of a severe body tic following a family disruption that the possibility of finding lost affect and the capacity for an integration of the psychic and somatic becomes available through the analytic process.

Hysterics indicate trouble with the body. As Bollas writes: "if a mother has under stimulated the infant, then auto-erotic will stand in for the lack of maternal sensorial care, but if the mother was deeply seductive, then the child will make an unconscious link between self stimulation and maternal love" (Bollas 2000, p. 31). But what if at the age one would expect the child to be developing psychosomatic theories of sexuality, the more pressing system is absence (through death) of the mother and absence (through breakdown) of the father. Then the natural territory of the play with mother's body and the development of the Oedipal triangle can become severely disrupted. It is this territory that I am interested in, and in particular the capacity to mourn as the prerequisite for the movement of bodily tic to be able to develop towards emotional accessibility.

A single man in his early thirties was referred with a long-standing obsessive-compulsive disorder. Some months before, the illness had increased to encompass a depressive ruminatory state together with suicidal ideas and a serious motor disturbance. He had been hospitalized for the previous three months, having quite violent and sudden involuntary movements, raising his hands suddenly above his head, moving his head from left to right violently with sudden twisting movements of his whole body. Despite being highly intelligent, he had coalesced his thoughts into a concrete idea that "one side of my brain is fighting the other side". He was very concerned that he might be gay despite his having many indications in the reality of his life to the contrary.

He enjoyed dating women and having sex with them and thought the idea of kissing a man abhorrent. Nonetheless, he had a delusional conviction that his destiny was to become homosexual. In addition, he had fleeting thoughts that he might be a woman.

He had been investigated by several psychiatrists and neurologists and variously diagnosed with obsessive-compulsive disorder, anxiety and depression, paroxysmal psychogenic movement disorder, and possibly cycloid psychosis. The inpatient treatment had failed to dent his symptoms; in fact, with an inability to look after himself or continue his professional work, life had been emptying out. The psychiatrists wanted him to have further treatment with "strong" antidepressants, lithium, and ECT. Instead, he came into five-times-a-week analysis.

Some years before, he had been in analysis, which had been of value in settling his obsessional-compulsive disorder. Despite a plethora of advice to beware of analysis on the grounds that it was likely to make him more ill, and even though also in conflict with a decision he had made never to go into analysis again, he decided to have a second analysis. This was another example of his obsessional state of mind, with a yes-no in reaction to analytic treatment. When Mr C. was two years old, his mother killed herself by hanging, soon after the birth of his younger sister. It seemed reasonable to think that she had been preoccupied for some period of time prior to her death, such that he had had very little freely available time with his mother as a baby. What quality of maternal care he was able to receive from her in such a short time is also unknown. Three years later, his father remarried. He always declined to talk about this early devastation. Instead, there was an emergence into the new family, which seemed strong and loving.

As a teenager, Mr C. was both indecisive and a perfectionist. In his early teens, he was very preoccupied with disease and often checked "for something bad in the corner of rooms". In his early twenties, he had his first depressive breakdown. Two years later, he began analysis for about four years, and in the latter part of this required hospital admission for five weeks due to increasing anxiety, obsessional thinking, and depression.

In the two years prior to his referral to me, his father suffered a very serious reversal in his successful business and for the first time had great financial difficulties. His stepmother became seriously ill physically, and a few months prior to his recent hospitalization his parents separated.

At the first consultation, he had gross choreaform movements and uttered streams of angry "yes-no". Sitting in a chair in front of a bookcase, he swung his head violently backward, yet each time he missed banging it hard by a hair's breadth. I took this as a serious sign that his gross movements had an underlying hysteria due to his unconscious capacity to not damage himself whilst indicating doing the opposite.

The failure of his brilliant father, for the first time, had devastated him. He also found his parents' separation terrible. Mr C. was a man who managed life by greatly idealizing his father in business and his parents in marriage. The devastation in his early life, with the sudden loss of his mother when he was two, had been a blanked-out subject which he was now unconsciously revisiting.

He told his story alongside a constant bodily performance of twisting gestures and shouting out "yes-no". He was exhibiting a major mental fragmentation that seemed to be embodied as an attempt to avoid any affect. Rather, it seemed the bodily contortions were meant to take the audience's mind, as well as his own mind, away from serious traumas, both recent and past, whilst simultaneously performing an enactment of them.

Intellectually, he thought that the idea that he was avoiding his feelings by embodying his conflict was probably correct. At the start of analysis, he was on the cusp of leaving hospital, anxious about looking after himself and returning to work. I offered him treatment on the basis that he would need to look after himself enough, be able to bring himself to and from sessions whilst commencing a return to work, initially for two periods a week. As his general functioning improved, his work slowly returned towards normal and he was able to move from the chair to the couch. His improvement was not from his desire to idealize our work, which was in fact often mocked, but rather his having to face a de-idealization of his family and professional life in the context of such reappearances in the transference. This was his ambivalence of both loving our work and, it became clear, this being his second analysis, that his simply thinking that our work was helpful was a form of resistance to deeper understanding. It did not do justice to his experiences, exemplified by the ambivalence contained in the constant yes-no expletives. In time, he began to understand his position better in terms of his ambivalence rather than having to know only that his father was wonderful in everything that he did. Similarly, if it were not the wonderful analysis, he would revert to an opposite position, indicating that I was useless compared to cognitive behavioural therapy.

A breakthrough came when he spoke about having a rope hanging in his living room and that he played daily with the idea of using it. I offered to look after the rope. Within a few sessions, he brought it to me to keep (temporarily) for him. This was a moment of trust and a linkage between us of concern that included destruction and the actuality that his mother had hanged herself. It was a moment of really taking something seriously and not prevaricating with an obsessional yes-no. It was also a moment when his past was connected to his present but held firmly in a new way, within the analytic relationship.

When he spoke of leaving his apartment with its hanging rope, it was a moment of testing me. Certainly, it was a shocking revelation, leaving me to ponder on whether, after any session, he would return home and hang himself. A case could be made for deciding at that moment that the patient was so suicidal that only an inpatient psychiatric setting would be sensible. And yet, he had lived with the rope hanging from the ceiling for a long time and had not harmed himself. The hospital as a place of safety belies the sad notion that it is not uncommon for suicidal patients to kill themselves on hospital wards, where they are usually observed and less often listened to. Mr C. was curious, at that moment, about how I would deal with his violent self. In a spontaneous interpretation, I offered care and a home for the rope. I offered to share the destructive object with him, without demanding something, such as he must give it to me, or must go to hospital. It was an offer to deepen our connectedness without my being frightened of his violence.

As months went by, he found he had specific thoughts and feelings in relation to his family and work that no longer needed to be balanced instantly by the opposite. As he started to feel particularly angry at various objects and moved away from an emotionally vapid balance, his stereotypy of movement diminished. He began to go to work every day and was able to think deeply within his professional expertise. This was something he thought he had irrevocably lost, and he was very grateful that his fragmented mind was showing signs of being able to have deep and connected thoughts again.

Theoretically, I thought that his gross body movements were a hysterical overlay to defend against affect. I decided not to speak about the lessening of the violent movements unless Mr C. did so himself. This was because I thought he was vulnerable to immediately doing the opposite; it was his usual way of obsessionally balancing himself as well as being aggressive to the other and avoiding affect. Gradually, he began to realize that he was not some sort of "puppet on a string" (a hanging man) and nor was he empty of feelings.

Clinical material

Mr C. began one session by saying that he now found that most of his strange movements mainly occurred when he entered my consulting room. Otherwise, he realized he was much freer in his body movements. After a pause, he added that he knew he could twist the truth. I decided to interpret that the twisting of the truth was also contained in his symptoms of twisted movements of his body. He said that there was a strain on his neck and wondered if he was gay or not. "Yes-no … I am obsessing." He felt he could turn his brain and twist it the way he wanted it. He could make it straight not gay even though he knew this was not how the brain worked. He thought that his will could move his brain and that the process had become particularly intense two days prior to his recent hospitalization. He wondered if he was lying to himself. He said that he took some thoughts about his life and then twisted the details to what he would have preferred them to be. He thought that gays were happy when they came out. He thought that his mind created the strange body movements: "I manipulate my mind. I don't question it all the time and although my life is better I will often have a tiny grudge. I want to play a happy world at work but everything is not amazing. I used to be like a rollercoaster, even when well. Moving—changes—sent me into panic. Hang on."

He thought that, recently, every time he had entered a difficult territory, such as a recent party he had given and a trip abroad, this had paid off. He now included his analysis in such a good category. I said, "You think that your mind tells the truth and at times it twists the truth". He knew that he didn't lie all the time, but he felt that he could not bear bad feelings and it was these that he twisted to be away from the truth. He felt that his feelings were just a step away from catastrophe and seemed always to be linked with disaster. "I suppose it was because my mother wasn't there. I was alone in dark rooms, terrified. My father said I would never play with the door closed. I always needed to see my father. I had no feeling of safety." I said that, "you also noticed how your father looked, especially if you thought father was suffering and in your mind you could twist fantasies in order to make your perceptions look as if your father was ok".

Towards the end of the session, he realized that recently he actually had to say to his father "go away" as he had helped his father enough at that moment. I said that this was new and different from the past; your mother went away and didn't return and you now dare say "go away". Yes, he replied, it is progress.

In this session, as the transference neurosis develops further, Mr C. connects, for the first time, his strange body movements and the clinical setting. His second statement was his idea that he could twist the truth. Mr C. is able to describe how, as a consequence of not being able to bear certain feelings because they place him on the brink of catastrophe, he is able to phantasize instead of having to reckon with that which he knows. Truth is disrupted as a protective mechanism from falling into the chasm of affect. Alongside, he also imagines that he is sexually twisted, as his body twists, in being homosexual or even being a woman who wants a man.

He continues, in the session, to describe his great fear: "I suppose it was because my mother wasn't there. I was alone in dark rooms terrified." The reality of his mother's total absence from his life when he was two years old, and perhaps even before that, includes an idea that nobody else was available to care for him. It is possible to imagine that he was treated with a bodily abruptness by the carer, in all likelihood his father, unused to such matters. His present jerky symptoms could contain a psychosomatic memory of the initial absence of his mother as well as the physical failure of his care that followed. His stepmother only arrived on the scene three years later.

Mr C.'s first breakdown happened when he was two, and the environmental loss, replaced by perhaps a much coarser physical caring, could not subsequently have been known about in any conscious way. Both the truth of his loss, and how he was possibly unwittingly poorly looked after as a consequence, return as the repressed found representation in hysterical bodily movements and ideas of his of being a woman. He identifies with the lost object although he is profoundly uncertain of any qualities of his mother, being more preoccupied by her death and its abrupt impact on his life, then and now. Utilizing such symptoms he also found a way of dealing with the fall of his father and the loss of his stepmother.

At the end of the session, Mr C. was able to tell his father to go away. Now he was beginning to own his own affect, including his anger towards his father for many things. He could only say this to his father by reaching the point of being able to know that his father, being away, would not also die. Now he could have a more alive relation to him with ambivalence and therefore with less need to contain his anxiety within psychosomatic defences. As this was the penultimate session of the term, I could have subordinated the direction of the free associations in the session to an interpretation pointing out his anxiety about the impending break from analysis. He had an idea of telling his father to go away similar to me telling him to leave my practice for a break. This clearly has a resonance, but its early interpretation only locates me at the centre of his world. Being able to dare push his father away with an unequivocal "no" is profound and is, of course, found, as it were, due to the transference tension close to the end of an analytic term. My point is the importance of locating analytic experience, then and now, at any moment in the analysis.

For most of Mr C.'s life, the happenings around the time he had with his mother and her sudden suicide when he was two years old, soon after the birth of his younger sister, were wiped out. The new family constellation became the family seemingly with no prior history that could be grasped or imagined. Mr C.'s early symptoms included look-ing with anxiety into the corner of rooms. Something on the edge of what was going on in his life constantly preoccupied him and developed into a system for dealing with the concomitant anxiety as his obsessional defences developed. In a sense, all was sufficiently balanced in his psy-chic life without history. On the surface, he was living his own life in his own house whilst having a high-powered professional career. Yet he had difficulty in being in a relationship with a woman. If a core part of his unconscious self was the life and early death of his birth mother, then all the solidity of his father's second marriage, from when he was five, including its love, did not address the point of absence. His mother went missing suddenly never to return. Subsequently, during his grow-ing up in the absence of talking about her and her meanings for him, his core emotional life was relegated to the corners of rooms and then covered up in the to and fro of obsessional thinking. Father was only seen as a wonderful kind-hearted character deeply caring for every-one. When father's world also began to disintegrate, suddenly Mr C.'s unconscious recourse was to move towards his own fragmentation. The separation of his parents was then a bombshell. He could no longer mentally hide in a flourishing family life. Suddenly, mother had disap-peared again, evoking the sudden loss of the original mother. Father no longer on a pedestal and mother absent required greater mental resources if the carapace over his emotional life was not to crack. The obsessional defences were arguably insufficient to deal with the new traumas and his body ego needed to be put at the disposal of bearing the weight of his mental avoidance.

Yet within the symptom is also the link to the solution. Mr C.'s body had been in a state of constantly and suddenly twisting itself. This was a motion rather than an emotion. It derived its power from twisting the truth. In addition, he would shout "yes-no" many times as if to show the ambivalent position as balanced when clearly it was not. The importance of the absent mother and collapsed father became significant in relation to Mr C.'s loss. Not only did his mother never appear again for him, but the two-year-old also had a psychically broken father in a state of loss. He had no memory of what happened in the three years from mother's death to his father remarrying. He did know that he called his stepmother "mother" as anything else would have been disloyal to his father. Even more so, it may have pitched father back into being broken by inviting the remembrance of his past.

As he noticed the return of his original traumas in the present tense of his family's difficulties, he began to forge a new relationship with his father. Instead of being instantly available to his father's summons, he began to realize that much of the relationship was superficial and immature. He began to realize that his father dealt with his own anxiety obsessionally; he needed daily or more reassurance from his son and it was valued only during the breath it took to utter.

Now he could begin a separation from father which, although still involving his love and care for him, also required Mr C.'s own selfhood and individuation. Mr C. had to painfully realize that his father often did not listen to him, hence the requirement for a repetitious formula described by the family as "listening to poor father". Similarly, he could begin to discern that some of his difficulty with girlfriends in the past was about his unconscious anxiety that they would suddenly leave him as mother had done. To prevent this, he invariably precipitated the leaving. One can consider such behaviour as containing both a killing of a girl-friend as well as protecting her from her own violence, like his mother.

It is possible to conjecture that his jerky body movements were an unconscious representation of his sexuality. Concern at being heterosexual was entwined with camp movements (noted also by the neurologist), as this meant for Mr C. that he was homosexual. Yet there seemed pretence in so far as his desire to be a woman also contained, alongside identification with women/mother, his loathing of them. It is somewhat well known that some men attempt to partially hang by the neck from a rope in order to increase masturbatory pleasure. At such a moment, sex and death are in close proximity.

In Mr C.'s case, in addition to the reasons for identifying with her, he would be identifying with his mother's form of suicide: an act that is rather more a masculine choice of suicide. Perhaps one way of understanding is that if mother kills herself utilizing an overtly physical and masculine design, then, in a confusional fragmentation, he can be a camp follower. Mr C.'s body bears witness to a psychosomatic state that is felt to be emotionally unbearable. As he said in the session, "hang on", and this is what he did with his own rollercoaster body movements. The aftermath of his mother's hanging necessitated his own hanging on.

His thoughts, not just of being gay, but perhaps really being a woman were an attempt unconsciously to bring his dead mother and absent stepmother alive as himself. He became, in some of his gay camped-up movements, the absent women that he longed for. His other identification with his mother is clear in his erecting a rope in his living room to have available as a concretization of her death by hanging. Giving up the rope made his affect more available, and he began to feel the present state of the double loss of mother's and family life. As he became more thoughtful about this and began to mourn, his body was required to twist less and less from truth. The rope is symbolic of a transference position that has several meanings. It represented a deep moment between the two of us, binding him to me, as in an unconscious umbilical connection. It also contained in the transference the beginning of his ability to engage some of his violent hate to the object (myself) without a re-killing.

At this point, one might wonder about the risk of his falling into a deep depression as the reality as well as the longevity of his fight against mourning emerged. This did not happen as it was mitigated by his realization that his mind was returning not just with feelings but with a capacity to think. By not having blank no-go areas in his mind, he could revitalize himself and feel more alive. Similarly, the bodily evocation of the re-evoked missing mother in the eighteen months of his present illness, with sudden wild movements towards and away from the person in dialogue, had diminished due to a revitalization of his imagination.

The return to normal body movements came from his ability to imagine beyond the bounds that he had until then placed around family life and idealized. His unconscious demanded that father needed to be preserved on high at all costs. He was the other parent who could still be present. The two-year-old and the child subsequently needed a damper put on the ordinary capacity to unconsciously destroy the parents in the age-specific development of magical-destructive omnipotence. Inevitably, this restriction leads to a diminution in the capacity to metaphorize. For Gubrich-Simitis, describing second-generation Holocaust survivors, the analytic treatment of severely traumatized patients involves trying to reach the trauma that remains unspoken, and thereby releasing the associative and imaginative capacities of the patient. She describes such psychological movement as being from "concretism to metaphor" in the clinical setting (Gubrich-Simitis 1984, pp. 301–319). That seems a valid way of thinking about Mr C., who presents with profound psychosomatic reactions in a mental setting rather devoid of imagination. At the start of analysis, his conflicts had no conscious connection with any history.

Perhaps his aggressive movements could be thought of as an intermediate position between concretism and metaphor, as an attempt to move his body to force possible other ways of understanding. The same would be valid for the yes-no repetitions, which clearly show him perseverating between two positions. In this, Mr C. had a willing ally, as his father too swept away thoughts and feelings about his first wife and family. Mr C. had a highly defended inner life with an unconscious fear and guilt over losing the object, and this was what made his obsessional defences so meaningful in the presence and absence of that which is missing.

In one sense, Mr C. could be understood as having a hereditary disorder by having, for instance, a genetic disposition to his father's obsessional state together with his mother's severe depression. Such a diagnostic direction totally leaves out any experiences, thoughts, and feelings throughout his whole life. Rather, it locates his actual life experiences to an annexe, whilst simultaneously taking any treatment hope away. It is important to remember that several psychiatrists had treated him with all manner of antidepressant and antipsychotic medication, to no avail. Psychoanalysis was able to restore hope to him.

The perfectly lovely relationship with a wonderful father was vacuous and was now replaced by Mr C. being able to offer real help to his father. Yet it came at the price of having to see his father's fall from grace and giving up supporting his father's constant wish for reassurance about the business. Realizing such dialogue was empty enabled

Mr A. to dare to decline to speak. This led to his having a more mature relationship with his obsessional father. Instead, he could give advice that required a degree of circumspection, with even the possibility of angering his father if he disagreed. Mr A. had moved from protecting his father from magical omnipotence to a more real position of being able to know his own hate.

Similarly, Mr C. moved from playing seriously in an identification with his hanging mother as her hateful gift to the family, to bringing the rope to be cared for transformatively by the analyst. The rope to hang is turned from a concrete fact in his daily life utilized to both torture and deal with unconscious guilt into a metaphor of linkage. It thereby becomes a rope that bound the two together, analyst and analysand, in daring to explore his early and present life beyond the rigid boundaries of his capacity to think.

His jerky movements as represented as a puppet on a string may contain an embodied hallucination of what he imagined happened to his mother when she killed herself. His tics point to an enactment of her suicide. Yet in addition to exposing bodily suicide, the act implies that the hanger is still alive. The tic addresses the imagined trauma to his mother, re-creates it in his own body as the only place for him to experience it, and concurrently keeps his mother and himself alive in the struggle.

It is remarkable that this behaviour began following the separation of his father and stepmother, a marriage that had lasted for all but five years of Mr C.'s life. The unconscious representation of losing his mother again, in the family atmosphere where such matters were not discussed, coalesced with the loss of his stepmother and the downfall of his father.

I now will look at the slight literature relating to tics in early psycho-analytic studies. In Ferenczi's paper on tics (Ferenczi 1921), he notes that he had never had a patient who came to analysis for the express purpose of curing tics. He explains the unconscious links between the bodily expressions as hysteria and paranoia, as in drawing unwanted attention to oneself in the grip of strange body movement. Such patients have to cope with their twisted body and expletives being seen by family, friends, and at work.

Ferenczi quotes the research of two physicians, Meige and Feindel, in their book *Tic, its Nature and Treatment*. They write that the starting point of a tic may be a hypochondriac self-observation.

"One day I felt ... a crack in the neck and at first I thought something had broken", said a patient, "To make sure I repeated the movement without noticing the crack, I varied it in a thousand ways and more violently. At last, I felt the crack again and this gave me real pleasure ... however the pleasure was soon disturbed by the fear that I had caused some injury" (Ferenczi 1921, p. 150). My patient too began his tic with a sensation that something had "plopped" in his head, "as if an evil clown had come out". It coincided with a thought that he would like to kill his sister. A week later, he found himself writing the name of his first analyst, and he spontaneously jumped. This was the start of the body tics. All this time, he was conflicted with thoughts about being "sucked back into his family" or being able to be more separate. In a certain sense, his dilemma was then managed by being hospitalized.

Ferenczi (1921) explained the mechanisms of the "mysterious leap from the mental to the physical" in the formation of hysterical symptoms. In conversion hysteria, the object memories repressed by psychic energy are used to reinforce and finally to "materialize" the difficult ego (body) memories associated with them. One can consider that this is one of Ferenczi's contributions to the development of the theory of hysteria following Freud and Breuer's early discoveries. For Mr C., enquiry after his mother, let alone mourning as he grew up, was a lost, forbidden subject. It was as if raising the topic would lead to father's collapse and even his loss too. This constellation had left Mr C. with an area of his mind devoid of being able to imagine.

Ferenczi's paper was discussed at a meeting of the Berlin Psycho-Analytical Society on 9 June 1921 and Abraham contributed a report (Abraham 1921, p. 323). Accordingly, he thought that the tic was a conversion symptom at the anal-sadistic stage. In 1925, Melanie Klein also wrote a paper in relation to Ferenczi's entitled "A Contribution to the Psychogenesis of Tics" (Klein 1925). In it, she describes the analysis of two boys aged thirteen and nine, and agrees with her former analyst that the tic is a masturbatory equivalent. Her treatment reveals the early object relations of genital, anal, and oral sadism on which the tic symptom is based. Whilst accepting that neurotic patients have masturbatory phantasies no different from patients with a tic, she was interested in discovering more specific factors. Klein finally relates the tic symptom with the patient observing and listening very early on in life to parental intercourse, and it is this that is converted into the physical manifestations of the tic as masturbatory phantasy enacted.

For my adult patient, the tic symptoms appeared in adulthood with no known early representation. The two-year-old's observation and/or imagining of his dead mother, together with its sudden and massive impact on his father and family life, becomes the psychosexual source of the phantasy material that eventually develops into tic symptoms. In this case, it is not only infantile sexuality but its relationship with absence, death, and the inability to mourn that my patient crafts into adult symptoms due to contemporary disturbances in the family, his parents' separation, and father's financial collapse. Yet there is a clear link, prior to his recent illness, between early life and relationships with girls, sexual difficulties, and homosexual anxiety.

Abraham and Torok write convincingly about a type of arrested memory that they describe as endocryptic phenomena (Abraham & Torok 1973). The hidden side of the vast majority of the so-called "psychosomatic" illnesses is actually the return, by way of pain, sickness, and physiological calamity, of the dead who are in mourning. This is so because the melancholic phantasy—the phantasy of empathy with the lost object who is bereft of me—is taboo (ibid., p. 162). They ask what happens when endocryptic subjects are visualized in melancholic phantasy. The only resolution available to them is to use their own body in a quasi-hysterical fashion. As Abraham and Torok state, "the deceased person is incorporated by the subject in this way, 'I carry in me someone who is dead and who cannot digest the fact of having lost me'" (ibid., p. 163).

From this perspective, the dead object unrealized or imagined has a task, which is to know that they have lost the subject. It is a neat reversal of the mourning process in which it is the one left alive who perforce has to miss the dead. The arrested development is stuck in the very requirement that the dead object needs to continuously know what it has lost in the alive person. This unconscious phantasy of the dead looking down in such an alive, so to speak, way is one of the possibilities linking unresolved mourning and hysteria.

Published in the same year as Ferenczi's tic paper, there is a poignant example of this structure in Proust's *Sodom and Gomorrah*. The author, in bending down to undo his boot, suddenly remembers that he has forgotten to remember his dead grandmother, "Then I thought I remembered that shortly after she died, my grandmother had said to me, sobbing, with a humble expression, like an old servant who has been dismissed, like a stranger: 'You'll allow me to see you sometimes

all the same, don't let me go too many years without visiting me'"
(Proust 1921, p. 163).

In a more recent session, Mr C. said, "I was always attracted to unstable women. I suppose I have been hanging on to my mother." I interpreted that he was describing in his language hanging on to a hanging mother, as a form of avoiding mourning. He replied that he was feeling *trauerlicht* and quickly realized that on speaking about his sad feelings, he had reverted to his mother tongue. He then remembered that his stepmother knew he needed psychological help when he was eight or nine years old. He had gone to a party in a school classroom. Everyone had gone by the time he arrived and he sobbed.

Mr C. was able to move in his free associations to hanging on to his dead mother, to speaking of sadness in his mother tongue, to remembering a childhood memory of crying when everyone was missing. Clearly, these are free-associative references back in time, unconsciously linking to when he was two years old and his mother disappeared. Such sequences enabled him to begin to invest in a new process of mourning. Not all causes of conversion hysteria contain such elements. However, a particular form of mourning is the undead subject, something that André Green has written about very evocatively.

The work continues, and the groundwork has been laid for the next stage of analysis. He has stayed away, more or less, from the frightening arena of a sexual relationship with a woman. His unconscious anxiety that soon after penetration one or other of the couple will have to be violent, or a "lust murder will need to happen", is beginning to be understood. Staying in analysis is a representation, in itself, of a developing capacity to stay and face reality. Nonetheless, the unconscious representations of the hanging mother are profound and will need to be worked through not just about the postcoital state but also when his partner becomes a mother herself. This will be a future test for the efficacy of the analytic process.

Despite a great deal of inpatient care, medication, and time away from work responsibilities, with the onset of intensive analytical treatment, his general hysteria and passivity in relation to the demands of ordinary life were able to change considerably over some seven months during that particular phase of the work. I expect this is due to his mind and capacity for free association, as well as his violent phantasies, being taken seriously. Mr C. was able to move from hysterical body movements to mourning for a dead mother and an idealized family.

CHAPTER FOUR

Trauma, psychosis, and regression: the psychoanalytic treatment of a schizophrenic patient

... I woke to find myself in a dark wood,
for I had wandered off from a straight path.

—Dante, *The Divine Comedy, Canto 1*

The issue of regression has always been a matter of intense controversy in the British Society. There has been much conflict around the idea that the analyst may be acting out his own difficulties towards the patient rather than being in the experience of part of the patient's unconscious object-relatingness. Much of the heated misunderstandings arise from where the analyst is located in the clinical scene. The analyst, watching the patient unfold his material and then interpreting it, is in a different locus from the analyst being alongside and together with his analysand. The difference is even more stark if the analyst expects and understands that the patient is "doing something" to the analyst, often in the negative sense, rather than inevitably being part of the exploratory analytic pair. A modern argument about the forces of regression wonders how the analyst can want to worsen the patient's already precarious balance by allowing such a direction to occur. As if such an analytic journey is too dangerous—or should the question be dangerous for whom? Yet for some analysts, regression has been imagined as the equivalent to the gratification of a warm cuddle between a mother and a baby in order to make things better. Regression seen from such a position is regarded as superficial and certainly not going deep in an analysis. Furthermore, it is linked to the anxiety that gratification is linked to dependency and that such a behaviour leads to the idealizing of the transference.

In this chapter, I will argue that for very ill patients regression becomes an essential analytic tool to enable that which cannot and must not be put into words to have a place in the process of the analysis. Such patients invariably are intensely alone, beyond daring to trust another person up to this stage in their lives. They also have a great fear of dependency, perhaps because of earlier assaults on their capacity to trust as children. They have a life that can be thought of as being barely alive, yet life is also held onto rather than suicide. Yet if regression becomes possible, the dependence that inevitably emerges is only a station on the path of really being an independent character.

Such very ill patients, if the Ferenczi-Balint view is acknowledged, require capacities in the analyst to be able to be in countertransference states of mind that may feel terrible, containing, as they do, aggressive and violent historical shards. These contain a mixture of what was done to the patient in early life, what was imagined to be done, and what was the defensive reaction, conscious and unconscious, to the other as destructive revenge. At times, this may lead to the patient feeling worse as well as the analyst feeling despair as if this is a warning to go no further along such paths. For both, it requires the letting go of the comfort of a known state of mind: for the patient, the sense of holding oneself through one's own defensive state, as the best, always available solution, despite its difficult consequences that have pushed him towards seeking analysis. For the analyst, it requires leaving the comfort of one's known understandings and theory and becoming more lost in what seem very deep waters. Such is the analytic journey that at times necessitates both in the couple holding their nerve, in order to see beyond the blackness.

Following Freud, regression was (and still is today) the essential concept for beginning to describe going back in time during an analysis. The patient, in a state of regression, finds themselves being within an experience that is in certain meaningful ways a re-experiencing of atmospheres and affects from his early object relationships. "Pathological regression" became a term used to conceptualize an understanding of the patient's recreation of scenes that may include early mental assault, which led to Ferenczi's concept of the defensive "atomization" (Ferenczi 1933, p. 165) of mental structures. This idea of atomization came from Ferenczi's thinking about a mind being unable to bear containing and holding on to the integration of thoughts, feelings, and history because of the intense painfulness of what would have to be known. Rather than just unconscious elements being split off, projected, and abandoned, in more severe pathology the mental structure itself fractures under the psychic strain and falls to pieces. For Ferenczi, this also had a protective function, in that the fragments still contained the many parts of the whole and the fragmentation enabled some capacity to retain the character of the individual, but analysis would be required to attempt to put the pieces back together in some new way. An analogy would be the restoration of a fractured stained-glass window or a fresco in pieces on the ground, which could be restored bit by bit to view. Accompanying this process was the need to discover techniques to both understand and, more importantly clinically, to emotionally connect with some patients who have spent their lives protecting themselves by existing without the other.

In the area of regression, Ferenczi's and Freud's views diverged. For Freud, regression needed to be understood and primarily interpreted, but for Ferenczi there was an additional emphasis on the being in and feeling of the experience. This was a shared experience that would involve both analyst and analysand. As Ferenczi wrote, "It definitely looks as if one could never reach any real convictions at all through logical insight alone; one needs to have lived through an affective experience, to have so to speak, felt it in one's body, in order to gain conviction" (Ferenczi 1912, p. 193). He believed that action and acting were not necessarily defensive or about resistance, but that through the reliving of an experience, repetition transformed remembering, leading to knowledge.

Ferenczi noted that the transference is a product of the combined unconscious intersubjectivities of the patient and analyst. With his interest in clinical work, he treated a group of severely ill patients. For those patients with profound early mental fracture, he writes:

> I have finally come to realize that it is an unavoidable task for the
> analyst: Although he may behave as he will, he may take kindness
> and relaxation as far as he possibly can, the time will come when he

will have to repeat with his own hands the act of murder previously perpetrated against the patient.

(Ferenczi 1932, p. 52)

This is an invitation for the analyst to realize that he may himself have to be in the traumatic centre of the patient's emotional life, with his own countertransferential affects in identification with the attacker. This is about understanding and not doing. Such a position anticipates Winnicott's radical idea that the "subject destroys the object, and the object survives destruction, such that the subject can use the object" (Winnicott 1971, p. 105). It is a call to carefully examine the contents of countertransference, in order to evaluate the possibility that it contains a re-enactment of early trauma. It also points to the vital importance that the analyst survives all assaults on the analytic position and maintains that stance without retaliation.

Following Ferenczi's pioneering work in describing the vicissitudes of what happens to subject and object in regression, Michael Balint further developed the clinical and theoretical field. He felt that just citing to the patient the connections between fixation and regression led only to a theoretical bleakness or even therapeutic stagnation. Balint valued Searles's, and in particular Winnicott's, studies of regression in the analytic setting. He was also heartened by Anna Freud's stress on the benign aspect of regression in her 1963 paper, "Regression as a Principle in Mental Development" (Freud 1963). He was particularly interested in the analyst's share in promoting or even provoking regression and in his technical responses to it. He felt that such matters were ignored by a literature that seemed to concentrate on Oedipal psychology. Balint believed that the understanding and the technical implications of the phenomena of regression belonged to an interaction between a particular analyst and a particular patient; in other words, the field of two-person psychology.

Ferenczi had discovered how many patients felt their parents to be remote and cold with them. He understood this in relation to the cold, detailed, analytic mirror position, which could easily become the re-enactment of the original trauma. This led him to re-examine technique in considering the idea of offering small areas of gratification in order not to re-enact such distance. Freud, for instance, had provided soup to the Ratman prior to a session, or as part of one, thus being aware of analytic atmosphere. Ferenczi discussed gratification in particular in his seminal paper "Confusion of Tongues" (1933), in which he developed the theme of professional hypocrisy; the analyst may well be thoughtful and clever with interpretations, but if this is applied at an emotional distance from the patient, as a doing to or a giving of something, then the analyst may be perceived, as perhaps the parent had been seen, at an emotional distance. As Ferenczi describes,

> The analytical situation—i.e., the restrained coolness, the professional hypocrisy and—hidden behind it but never revealed—a dislike of the patient which, nevertheless, he felt in all his being—such a situation was not essentially different from that which in his childhood had led to the illness.

> (Ferenczi 1955, p. 159)

This is the meaning of Balint's concern for analysis to reach an interpenetrating mix-up with the analyst being in a moment of emotional authenticity.

However, what Ferenczi did not bring into the picture, or know enough about at that time, was the stickiness of sadomasochistic resources in the patient, who might then abuse his offer of kindness. This was especially so with the difficult (borderline psychotic) patients who were referred to him. Ferenczi was confronted by the movement of pulling away from and empathy towards the patient, with such states sometimes changing quickly, within moments, in a session. He realized that the analyst's mental state is as important in elucidating the status of the patient's mind as the associations of the patient. Balint acknowledged the counterbalance in every analysis of the forward and backward motion of countertransference in our internal sensations of cold and warmth towards the patient, the meaning of this historically, and its impact on the here and now. In examining the concept of trauma, it is interesting to see how both Freud and Ferenczi conceptualized the idea. Freud concentrated on what was happening in the individuals—their ontogeny and sexuality. Ferenczi's focus, in addition, was on the individual's relationship to the world around and their responseto the changing environment. This was the beginning of the description of objects and their relationships—the new field of object relations. Whilst Klein's second analyst, Karl Abraham, has been regarded as an early influence on the development of her object relationship theories, her first analyst, Ferenczi, is usually unacknowledged in her theoretical development. Ferenczi encouraged her early work with children. Klein cites Ferenczi, in her preface to *The Psychoanalysis of Children*: "It is to him [Ferenczi] that I owe the foundations from which my work as an analyst developed" (Klein 1932, p. 11).

The field, as envisioned by Ferenczi, consisted of the unconscious affective relationships between the individual and the parents, including the parental couple's relationship as imagined and internalized. In addition, there are the lateral relations with siblings, those present and those only imagined, and their impact on the couple. Which child is imagined to be, or actually is, more or less favoured, and why, can become very important areas of mental life that will be repeated, as repetition is found in the imaginary. It was as early as 1935 that Balint had urged that more attention be paid to the development of object relationships. Describing the environment of the clinical relationship, Balint connected his ideas with Anna Freud's "need-satisfying object", Bion's "container-contained", and Winnicott's "good-enough mother", "primary maternal preoccupation", and the "holding function" of mother. Balint expected that the real problem is not about gratifying or frustrating the regressed patient, but about how the analyst's response to the regression would influence the patient–analyst relationship and, by it, the further course of treatment. Balint thought that it was inept to increase the power of the analyst by satisfying the patient's expectations. But, if satisfaction occurs not by increasing inequality, but by creating an object relationship in the pattern of "primary love", he thought it was worthy of being seriously considered.

Balint's work on regression culminated in his publishing *The Basic Fault* (1968). For him, the ability to obtain something good, which the baby or child had experienced too little of, might become available in the analysis. It led him to hypothesize an analytic direction which could then lead to new internal character changes—ego development which he called a *New Beginning* (Balint 1968, p. 132). In the state of new beginning, an increase in symptoms led to an increase in tension, which led to a moment of gratification of particular urges, which could lead to a tranquil, quiet moment of wellbeing. He thought that all such new beginnings happened in the transference, leading to a change in the patient's capacity to love and hate with a lessening of anxiety. Whilst the idea that the ego could develop through analysis was Freudian, Balint's title, containing such hope for change, has an idealizing quality. Balint called the new beginning an "arglos state", describing it as "a constellation in which an individual feels that nothing harmful in the environment is directed towards him and at the same time nothing harmful in him is directed towards his environment" (Balint 1968, p. 135). Rather than this being a guileless, innocent, and simple state, it can be regarded as a pre-paranoid state. For Balint, there was a crucial move away from Freud's idea of regression as entirely inside the patient's mind, and instead the new beginning was about a two-person psychology. "As development of object relationships was not a fashionable topic of the day, hardly any notice was taken of my findings, although I reported about them repeatedly" (ibid., p. 135). At times in the analysis, the analyst just has to be there as a substrate, like—to take Balint's analogies—being the air in our lungs or the water outside the fish, which is also flowing through its gills. It is a description of the analyst as substance. Balint is describing regression as benign. He separates it from malignant regression with its constant demand for addiction—like gratification, which is only in service for the purpose of demanding more.

Balint was interested in what he perceived as confusion within the concept of regression. One example was a state of withdrawal in regression, which, he noted, had been examined in Winnicott's idea of "being alone in the presence of the analyst" (Winnicott 1958, p. 34). Balint observed that some patients could be almost entirely absorbed in the area of their own creation. Overall the subject was so complex that different aspects could easily be picked out from the whole, as if they were the more worthy of attention, leading to a fragmentation of understanding of the term in itself. This is like the parable of a blind man describing an elephant only by the part he is touching at that moment. He described a "going back to something primitive to a point before the faulty development started and at the same time discovering a new better way of functioning" (Balint 1968, p. 131). Regression was for the sake of progression. Yet his concept of "basic fault" was too simplistic a term to describe a multiplicity of points of trauma in the early life of a person and their development in the world of internal object relationships due to an/the environmental setting when the baby was growing up. Like other theorists, he divided the field into benign or malignant regression.

Balint was very wary about the analyst being perceived as omnipotent. It is easy to see that this modern technique of interpreting transference first must lead to a picture of the world consisting of a rather insignificant subject confronted with mighty knowledgeable and omnipresent objects who have the power of expressing everything correctly in words, an impressive example of whom is the analyst. Balint was keen to point out the oral dependence that would follow if this was taken too far, and described how during treatment conducted in such a way, nearly all transactions between patient and analyst happen through the medium of words which reinforces the oral aspect of the clinical situation. This led him to be interested in silence in the clinical setting.

> I have experimented with the technique that allows a patient to experience a two-person relationship which cannot, need not, perhaps even must not, be expressed in words, but at times merely by, what is customarily called, "acting out" in the analytic situation. I hasten to add that all these non-verbal communications, the acting out, would of course be worked through after the patient has emerged from this level and reached the Oedipal level again—but not till then. At the Oedipal and even at some of the so-called pre-Oedipal levels a proper interpretation, which makes the repressed conflict conscious and thereby resolves the resistance or undoes a split, gets the patients' free associations going again; at the level of the basic fault this does not necessarily happen. Interpretation is either experienced as interference, cruelty, unwarranted demand or unfair impingement, as a hostile act, or a sign of affection, or is felt so lifeless, in fact dead that it has no affect at all.

> (Balint 1968, p. 175)

Interpretation is available for when the patient emerges from the deeply regressed state, or begins to emerge, as a means of bringing understanding into being with the primitive affect of the regression. However, now the patient has experienced a different way of being with the other, of being psychologically held and contained by the psychic dimensions of the analytic room, time, and space.

These concepts are about trying to make contact with patients who have had good reason to be extremely wary of such possibilities.

What follows is a part of a case study describing the clinical details of what I have just been describing in theory.

Mrs B.—some clinical material relating to a schizophrenic analysand

This material comes from the analysis of a middle-aged schizophrenic woman who was in six times weekly psychoanalysis for some years. The extra session on a Saturday became the means of underpinning enough of a holding state for the patient not to need to continually regress in a serious way in the long gap between Friday and Monday. Also, it averted the need for the patient to enact leaving analysis, unconsciously perceived as abandonment, by becoming so ill as to require psychiatric admission. The description of the clinical work directs attention towards an attempt to be in touch with some of the profoundly difficult states of pathological regression of the patient, together with some thoughts on technique in relation to the position of the analyst.

Mrs B. had been in the care of psychiatrists for many years. They had diagnosed her as schizophrenic during several periods of hospitalization. The patient was usually in such a regressed state in the consulting room that she eschewed the couch, opting to sit on the wooden floor in a far corner of the room from me. For much of the time, she sat in silence with her head hung low. Despite seeming to be indifferent to being in the session, she acutely observed, despite giving an appearance to the contrary. Perhaps surprisingly, outside the consulting room she held an important professional position. There, her ideas and concern for others' care was well known in the community and she seemed much respected. Yet this carapace was instantly shed on entering the analytic space.

To begin with, I shall describe a common situation occurring in this analysis in order to examine the difficulty of dealing with a verbally silent patient clearly manifesting intense affect. The following description is not from one particular session, but it is a description of a common atmosphere when being in the consulting room with her. (I will write partly in the present tense as a way of being in the moment with her and as a format for bringing the material to life.)

The patient moves from the doorway that she has entered to the nearest corner of the consulting room. She places herself like a naughty child who comes to be punished, often meaning that, for her, the excesses of violence and sadism in the night dictate that she must be in that position. In addition, she may kneel in an attitude reminiscent of prayer, for forgiveness, for salvation, or as a pastiche about how useless is, in the analysis, anticipation of the next night's cruelty. Whichever it is, as a particular start to a session, it is with such a range of possibilities that the patient begins.

I sit quietly waiting, and gradually I feel the patient gazing at me—to gauge my mood state, to see whether I am perhaps a little safer to be with, or whether to take my silence as an irritation. Meanwhile, from her state I sometimes have a hunch about what damage happened to her the previous night. If the latter, I seem often to be correct in my thoughts about the physical harm that she has done since the previous session. At this time in our work together, in between sessions, she takes a sharp carving knife and deliberately slices her upper arms, sometimes her breasts, and explores her vagina and anus with the knifepoint. After such attacks, the way she sits on the floor or in a corner is a silent indication of the soreness of her body.

Usually, if she tells of such events, she speaks in an affectless manner and the patient remains surprised that I am affected by the horror of that activity. To her, she has banished feeling and is nothing and worthless. Thus, it is an activity that is of no consequence to, or for, her. It is a piece of enacted sadomasochism that she believes has nothing to do with herself. In time, she was able to recognize the internal battle. The force inside her tells her to cut, implying that she will obtain relief. She fights the cruel direction by thinking about analysis, her analyst, of the room we work in, and by holding pieces of gravel she has taken from my driveway. The fight is won or lost. If she fails to draw blood, the battle for survival the next night is heightened, seemingly to demand a blood sacrifice.

The analyst is placed on a tightrope in relation to such material. If I am silent, the patient is left to think that I too do not mind the cutting of flesh, and may even ignore it, as does the patient (as previously described in Chapter One). Also, the silent analyst may be perceived as being silent like the mother who did not speak up against what her husband was doing to the child, and thus be hated by the patient for not helping. On the other hand, if I speak logically with an interpretation about cruelty in relation to the patient–analyst couple, it may be understood in an intellectual way, but the patient will still be left with the great problem of why there is a need for repetition. The patient may begin to feel that she does not hate the analyst, differentiating him for a moment from her father in the transference. Yet what really matters is whether she thinks she can observe the analyst as indifferent to what is going on. The patient is able in the silence to push and pull the material and her observation on what might be understood by her and me, in many directions.

It seems essential that such a patient is able to begin to see the pain she is actually able to emotionally inflict onto the other. Hence, the slow surreptitious looks and glances at the analyst to see his face and posture. The clinical work often seems to be in the following arenas of unconscious object relationships. Is the patient in a room with a primary loved father in the transference? Is the transference about a sadistic bully, attacker, and rapist, whom the patient has to be very careful of inciting? Is the patient, in the transference, the child who is in identification with the cruel father she is also tormenting? This would require the analyst to be in the position of voyeur. Furthermore, it is possible within the complexity of ideas to think all this from the opposite psychic position that the analyst is at the behest of a bullying mental assault: all vertices need to be thought about and, in time, interpreted.

One essential clinical task, then, is reality testing so that the patient may be able, perhaps for the first time, to be in a room with a man who is not going to assault her. Thus, her old nostrum that "all men are the same" can begin to break. Depending on such variables in the atmosphere of the room, the rest of the session follows. If the patient detects a cut-offness in the analyst, the session stays turgid and empty. The patient feels absent and the analyst is left to wait. The patient may perceive the affect in the analyst, which may be true, as inevitably the analyst has feelings at the assault the patient persists in making on them both. She may then go over to a painting above the couch and examine the gap between that and the wall. In particular, she seemed to be looking for a safe place between the picture and the wall in order to project a fragile ego in anticipation, in her mind, of the next assault. It is as if the patient had found refuge on high. She is then at one with the gods and can look down at the scene of what mere mortals do to and with each other, and that is enough for her to feel a little bit safer.

If the patient detected—by my posture or my interpretation or the tone of my voice—something that suggested I was with her and had some understanding of her, the session becomes very different.

Tears trickling down her face are at first ignored by her before sadness encroaches. She may be in a frame of reference in which she begins to know again that two persons need not only be about a violent sado-masochistic relationship. Now she has to experience a deeper pain and a pain that cannot be relegated to nothing with just a cut. This is the pain of experiencing reality that is not just some night time phantasm. At this point, she can be very sad, deeply distressed, and depressed at the knowledge of her awful history as a victim. This state of mind is very hard for her to maintain for long, but when in such a state, the analyst has a patient more in touch with reality. Being in touch with extremely painful affect had been warded off, until now, by splitting mechanisms, which eschewed any connections between then and now.

Ferenczi struggled with the problem of masochistic repetition:

> If the analyst succeeds in creating a conscious link between the delight and unpleasure in a specific situation that really existed, the compulsive character of masochism then ceases to operate, to be replaced by rationally justified capacity to endure unpleasure for the sake of the advantages anticipated in the future.

(Ferenczi 1932, p. 31)

Instead of constantly returning to the masochistic pleasure, which the onlooker finds so terrible, the analysand may learn to forgo such well-known and entrenched psychic defences. The reality of such a painful psychic state with its horrid antecedent history can then come to be known and felt by the patient, rather than just projected into the other as being the cruel onlooker, allowing other possibilities to open out in the future rather than just masochistic repetition. The problem is that Mrs B. does not feel she has any future, thus why does she need to change? She has children, but she has repressed the possibility that she has any effect on them, as she has repressed the idea of her having any effect on her parents or they on her.

So far, the clinical atmosphere has served particularly to illustrate the view of two-person psychology in relation to the regressed patient. How the analyst responds and is perceived by the patient is technically crucial to whether there is an increase in the difference between the two, especially with an increase in omnipotence, or a lessening of tension as the past ceases to be re-enacted by the working couple. This leads to the possibility of a benign experience in the regression and a move towards the development of a depressive state.

I will now describe some more of Mrs B.'s behaviour and states of mind. The patient often starved herself. She banged her head, cut and excoriated her body, and attempted to cover up the damage under her voluminous clothes. She over-washed and generally had such contempt for her body, preferring to have no skin, or that only her mind should exist. Her anxiety at both swallowing solid food and defecating could be understood as a rejection of such an orifice perceived as a perverse sexual place that she needed to wipe out. After much work was done in examining her difficulty in eating solid food, one example of counter-transference horror followed. Mrs B. arrived for her next session with much satisfaction showing on her face. With spite, I was informed that she had indeed attempted to swallow something solid. She had left the consulting room at the end of the previous session and on her way out, in the garden, had found some dog faeces to eat. The reader may readily appreciate the sadomasochistic attack and its humbling influence on the analyst. What followed was an exploration of whose shit she had imagined eating—she thought it was from my dog, meaning my shit with all the unconscious confusion of good food and excrement, mouth and anus, herself and myself, creativity versus paranoid attack. All the while, I was being constantly observed as to how I was experiencing this event and whether I would be able to bear the psychic pains. Could I really hold on to the idea that psychoanalytic work was creative and mutative rather than just a load of shit that only deteriorated her at best or at worse just had no effect on her whatsoever. All such thoughts and feelings required patient elaboration in words and sentences, in order for her to discriminate, to realize that the other, in the room with her, was different from what she had been so very used to. One way that a child, continually and unremittingly assaulted both mentally and physically, can survive is to signal to herself and another that nothing existentially matters at all. In the light of this, eating shit as if it is of no consequence is a powerful defensive tool.

Mrs B. dreamed and/or hallucinated, often vividly and invariably about some extreme attack that someone was doing to someone else. She was not necessarily the victim or the victimizer, but she was often the onlooker, and there seemed to be no escape from the repetitive horror. One way of reading this case, therefore, would be as a psychotic intensification of Freud's "A Child is Being Beaten", with the affect in the object relationships drastically increased and concretized. Very often, the patient discovered in the morning that she had enacted some ghastly action following or during a dream or hallucination. An example of this was a dream in which someone was cutting someone and when the patient awoke in the morning, she found that her body had actually been cut quite viciously with a pin or a piece of glass. Often, the attacking object had been unconsciously left around, in order to be used in the subsequent attack. The assaults by the patient on the analyst, who listened to such horrific material, were accepted by the analyst amidst sufficient boundaries. This was to enable the patient to know the reality of needing to be alive and to survive and to bring herself to analysis. In time, Mrs B. gradually realized that I could survive her assaults and that I was not a mechanism. She was then able to develop feelings about the assaults. The cutting of her body, which she had done since the age of six and for many years nightly as an adult, became a much rarer event. For such change to happen, the patient had to be able to begin to look at her blackness, her vicious repetitive dream world, her psychotic states, and her denial of such a process, in order to know her private trauma at the hands, we both suspected, of paedophilic parents.

Her intense aggression could be viewed now as identification with both parents. As the object of her attacks moved in the transference from her body to the analytic process, she was able to begin to see and feel the pain in me and also in her sense of concern for the other, and in time, gradually, herself. For someone who trained herself hardly to exist, this was an achievement.

As Winnicott has noted, for some patients the only way of reaching an understanding of what took place is not to remember but to be mad in the analytic setting. Such a patient unconsciously organizes delusional transference and the analyst accepts this and tries to understand it.

The following vignettes from two specific pieces of material are, first, about sexuality and, second, about Mrs B.'s dream life.

The patient began with some material from when she was five or six years of age, at which time she first remembered beginning to have a conscious phantasy that she wished she were a boy. She thought that if she could pull her labia enough, her genitals would develop into a penis. She had an omnipotent thought that if she wished hard enough then it would happen. She experimented by urinating whilst standing up. All this took place in the extreme fear of being found out by her parents. It seemed that such a phantasy was a form of defensive thinking in order to escape sexual abuse, which by now we both were convinced was at the core of her history. In the clinical material, the nature of the conflict between actual sexual abuse and destructive, defensive constructions becomes more clarified, but at this moment our shared "madness" was generated by clinical progression of the treatment. I think the unconscious idea behind such phantasy may be that "if I am a boy, my father will not want to abuse me, therefore I shall make myself be one of those and life will be better". I think it is likely that such a construction was shattered some years on, when she spoke about her brother being invited or forced by the parents into the paedophile circle (of which she was already at the centre) to have sex with my patient, his sister. I think the shattering of her mind, at this particular point, led to that defensive structure moving into a psychotic arena. Now she had a powerful enduring thought, at certain times, that she did have an erection. Although she knew intellectually about her anatomy, she could not disconnect the psychotic thought that she was a potent man. She was thus able to seemingly defend herself from assault by being the character with penetrative activity rather than having to be on the receiving end of being penetrated. This was certainly enacted by putting some sharp point into her skin, her anus, and her vagina, to prove the power of her psychotic construction and her contempt for her body in identification with her paedophilic parents.

From such reconstruction, one would need to think about psychotic manifestations being the outcome of a mental state developed from previous actual trauma. We do no justice to the disruption done to the mind, its atomization and reforming together in a psychotic state, by just naming it as an example of the irreducible "death drive". Such mental disruption clearly involves huge amounts of aggression, both towards the subject and the object. Nonetheless, if this is not analysed in great detail, in my view, then the concept of death drive can appear to be just a name to cover the gap in knowledge. In this context, I am in agreement with Jonathan Lear's view in his book *Happiness, Death and the Remainder of Life* that, "The theory of the death drive makes it look as though it is offering a real theory-linking aggression up to other phenomena and forces—but it is only a seductive gesture in the direction of theory" (Lear 2000, p. 88). Whilst the patient's perceptual state that I have been describing is clearly in the realms of aggression, just stating that as a descriptive interpretation, including "look what you are trying to do to me", belies the immense possibilities of a re-enactment of history and the move to Balint's crucial possibility of a new beginning of object relationships. Otherwise, there is only repetition. Lear continues his argument by drawing attention to the possibility of the *Fort-Da* game performing a state of being, stuck in between: "Only when the game is established will the loss be a loss for him" (ibid., p. 92). The loss has to be experienced for Mrs B. being between *Fort* and *Da* as a cogent description of her inability to process self and other and instead living in a constant in-between world where nothing matters and nothing really exists.

The child who was observed throwing the cotton reel out of the cot and then hauling it back again, in a losing and finding game, was Freud's grandson Ernst aged eighteen months (Freud 1920, p. 12). Between the throwing out of the object, accompanied by the idea of "gone" (*Fort*) to its return with the word "there" (*Da*) is an economy of pleasure in the absence of the object, mother. The game, played over and over, is an attempt at mastery over an unpleasure such as the child being alone. However, suppose that in the structure of the game, the cotton reel, either thrown out or returned, functions purely as a mechanical action that neither provides real mastery nor pleasure. Often, the repetitious and negatively reiterative behaviour patterns of the patient provide a masochistic solace precisely because of their sense of emptiness and desolation. It is a motion of despair, a comment, as it were, that nothing can be done, then, now, and in the future. The original possibilities of the cotton reel as play turn instead to the reality that play is not possible. Analysis becomes a means of enabling the (re)establishment of the internal structure that *Fort-Da* represents, allowing the capacity of mastery and its relinquishment to begin to emerge alongside playing. If this happens, the patient may emerge to know the possibilities of the other in the room, a move away from hopelessness towards hope contained in the dyad. This requires courage, in case, alongside this positive direction, there is also a return to the sadomasochistic nightmare of real early torture of some children. I am arguing that some clinical conditions, psychosis and in particular schizophrenia, have roots in previous early actual traumas, both physical and mental. The idea of the death drive is not a sufficient explanation for the complexity and brutality of these events and their aftermath. An intellectual knowledge of the possibility of the destructive instinct is a very poor substitute for finding it within the experiences of the analyst–analysand. Yet re-finding the aggression behind the repetitious emptiness in much of the clinical material leads to a re-finding as capacity to play inside oneself and with the other, which can develop into clinical improvement. A further discussion on the death drive will continue in Chapter Five.

Dream life and the schizophrenic

In the next vignette, Mrs B. was five minutes late for the session. She apologized, saying that the traffic was very intense. Then she hovered at the end of the couch for seven or eight minutes silently. Eventually, I interpreted that despite her apology for being late, she seemed some-what unmoved in her silence for several more minutes beyond that. She said she did not know what to say and that everything was a mud-dle. Then she told me that she had woken up from a dream. This in itself was unusual, as it was often very difficult to know whether she was having auditory and visual hallucinations when she was awake at night, or whether she was dreaming. This time, it sounded as if she was describing a dream.

It consisted of her feeling very frightened because a large funnel was chasing her. She was able to explain to me that her anxiety was that the point of the funnel which was nearest to her was actually going to be put over the whole of her. She thought this was rather silly. My pri-vate thought was that she was being chased by a combined genital, as an example of her genital confusion. It happened that the penis part was facing her but equally menacing was the opposite side, the vagina. However, this in itself seemed to be a progression from her feeling in other dream states that she had a penis attached to her body. This dream construction, at least, was separate from her whilst trying to attack her back.

It was also unclear why it was so frightening to be taken inside the funnel because if she went into the point, she would come out the other side. I interpreted this and she agreed. She then winced and remem-bered that when she was a little girl, her father would put her in the bath, place a funnel between her legs in her vagina and, attaching it to the taps, he would scald her with boiling water. She said this was the only time that she knew about the use of a funnel other than using it to put oil in a car. I interpreted that she was remembering the cruelty that her parents did to her and, in particular, to her body, and that she very often was like them in being very cruel to her own skin. She said, with a little voice, that she knew.

There was a pause. I said that I thought that her fear of the funnel might represent her coming through the front door, the funnel part, into the vestibule and then coming into my consulting room, which, at that time, was a large room in a barn with a high ceiling rising to an apex, which could also be an unconscious motif for the funnel. If this was so, then she actually was coming in through the point of the funnel, as my consulting room represented the widest part and she was frightened of that and our work. There is a clear implication of sexuality to such a description, yet I was reluctant to interpret it in that way as I felt that she was in a more primitive state of mind.

She said it was very frightening coming into the room, but also she thought that perhaps it could help. She then became rather frightened, still standing at the end of the couch and said that the words "paradise lost" had come to her mind, but it was silly. I said maybe she was in touch with the lost paradise when she imagined she was inside her mother and that ever since being born she had lost paradise. She then said that other fragmentary thoughts were on her mind. One, in particular, was the word "domino". She couldn't understand why that word came to her mind. I interpreted that maybe it was next to the word "domination" which she was not allowed to say. At this point, she said "shut up" in a menacing voice to me and to an internal imago that something must not be revealed. I said she knew the word "domination" very well because she had been subject to it as a child. In our work together, she saw me as dominating her at times, and I certainly felt her as dominating me, such as in the silence for several minutes at the beginning of the session when it seemed that she was in control. She began to cry and again said in a vicious tone "shut up" and then, "will I be helped with all this?" I said that behind her was a couch and on the couch was a blanket and, if she used those, there could be a sense of her being looked after for a few minutes, and then, the image of the funnel would be something that could look after her which she would also have to leave at the end of the session. Mrs B. was then able to lie on the couch, cover herself with the blanket, adopt the fetal position, and seem to be in a more peaceful and quiet repose until the end of the session. This had never happened before.

The muddle at the start of the session led to the remembering of a dream. The idiom of the attack, with all its concomitant anxieties and pleasure, was experienced in the transference. The experience contained in the dream and taken up in the transference led to a movement from paranoia to a remembering of early trauma. Or from psychosis via regression, to a position of understanding in the analyst and the patient that enabled the patient to cry and be in a depressive state whilst being cared for.

If the analytic technique is preoccupied with neurotic defences and neurotic mechanisms, it may avoid connection with psychotic processes. If one is interpreting as if the psychotic process is neurotic, it is quite likely that interpretation will fail when the patient is functioning in the area of psychosis. It is such confusion in this area that can lead to treatment failure.

In the psychotic arena, patients may not be able to hear and accept interpretation and digest and work it through. A relationship between two people in a room may not even exist. It is possible that one's sentences and interpretations are not heard as words but as things (cf. Freud's differentiation between word presentation and thing presentation; Freud 1915). The patients may not know that another person is even in the room with them. When the analyst does speak, the patient may perceive the sentence as a device to penetrate, so care is required in imagining which part of the body receives such things in a state of pathological regression. This is particularly relevant with those patients who really have been attacked and sexually assaulted earlier in their life.

Winnicott postulated a process in which something awful was actually seen by the child, which led to a de-hallucination in which it was covered over. Subsequently, a series of hallucinations begins to fill up the hole produced by the scotomization. He described such a process as being compulsive in that it had to be repeated again and again. As I described in the beginning of this chapter, some patients need to be psychotic in the transference in order to arrive at memories of a very disturbed and distressing kind, which belong to an earlier time. In other words, the psychosis is the blackness concealing early severe trauma as well as the hallucinations which express it and which are the source for understanding and interpretation.

For Mrs B., being in the consulting room was felt at times as being in the place where sexual assault took place. It was both of us surviving the immense pain of being again in the moment of the trauma that eventually enabled construction of the past. Together, we discovered near unimaginable aggression that had been done to her as a child by her parents and other paedophilic adults, constantly repeated as well as seemingly disconnected from the patient's apparent history.

To be alive, to anticipate advantage of the future with hope, must mean that she has to be in touch consciously with her past history. Instead, the patient had been left in a place in which there is an immensely painful physical and mental repetition, but at the same time repudiation, of such a state.

Ferenczi writes:

> I know from other analyses that a part of our personality can "die", but though many parts can survive the trauma, it wakes up with a gap in its memory, actually with a gap in the personality, since this is not just a memory of the actual death struggle that has selectively disappeared or perhaps has been destroyed but all the associations connected with it as well.

> (Ferenczi 1932, p. 79)

Patients often have a phantasy that if they are told what is going on, then all the difficult stuff will cease. If the patients have already given themselves up to death, they have no need of memory, which exists only when one knows one has a future. This is a very different understanding of death than the death drive. By this, I mean that many patients with horrific early trauma have one solution to deal finally with the immense psychic pain—that is, to kill themselves. Ferenczi is struggling to acknowledge unconscious ambivalence in such patients who do not commit suicide but rather suppress being alive in their life as a way of managing to continue. Partly being dead, as in a flattened affect, enables the true self, as Winnicott called it, to survive. Analytic treatment makes conscious the repressed memories and deep psychic pains, eventually enabling mourning of life until now (knowing about the "dead bits" of oneself), with the possibility of then being freer to live an alive life.

The world of Mrs B. was full of auditory, visual, tactile, and kinaesthetic hallucinations, which seemed to be fragments of previous real attacks, returning to haunt her in the emptiness she created by wiping out the offer of a real creative life. There had been such a massive breakdown of trust that the patient's need for absolute control of the real world left her in a psychotic dream world. This attempt at mastery achieved the opposite as the destructive imagery became the dominant culture of her mind and one that she often trusted in more than her analysis.

Whilst remaining alive, such patients can be understood, in André Green's memorable idea of the "dead mother" (Green 1986) as tending the shrine of the mother. Such mental structures maintain unconscious connectedness with mother, who neither seemed to care nor offer enough concern or love. For Mrs B., mother was the perverse attacker who penetrated her and also did not protect her from father's penetration. She identified with the negative aspects of mother and thus kept mother alive in a perverse shrine, where she worshipped the non-changingness of their lives. Breaking free meant a move towards an emotional life that included mourning, both the mother she had and hated, as well as the mother she wished to have and did not. A deep aspect of the death-destructive drive is to not let such a mother complex die. It is a profound dynamic that binds the analysand sadomasochistically with their objects in order for nothing to change. It contains the phantasy that by staying still, not moving physically and psychically, one will not be perceived by the aggressive penetrating object and so will continue to just survive. At the same time, it allows the potential for identifying with the aggressor. At this point, the question is about whether one harms another, as was done to oneself, or protects the other by damaging oneself physically. Self-harm enables a destructive play that re-enacts early attacks received whilst simultaneously protecting the other and disidentifying with the aggressor. Identifying and disidentifying simultaneously is the complexity of this aggressive clinical state.

Destructiveness and countertransference

The psychoanalysis of a psychotic patient is a severe challenge to the integrity of the analyst's capacity to bear knowing the thoughts and, more importantly, the feelings that lie buried within the auditory, visual, and tactile hallucinations. Sometimes the analytic task consists of having the patience to uncover the horrid traumas, such as exhuming dead bodies with a gradual exposition of how terror came about. No matter how ghastly it is for the onlooker, it needs to be managed. However, the atmosphere of the analytic position is that unconsciously the patient expects the severe assaults to be repeated by the analyst. Thus the paranoia is enacted through the patient's great fear of the analyst. Though the analyst does not physically touch the patient, the patient will feel the emanations of assault, having projected them on the analyst in order for them to be returned, yet again, against the patient, as paranoia becomes the central scene of the work canvas.

To complicate matters even more, the patient, having identified with the aggressor(s), verbally, and sometimes physically, attacks the analyst. Of course, such material is a communication, enabling the analyst, being in the transference in the position of the young patient, to feel the pain, terror, and dread of that which the patient felt was done to them. That said, one needs to bear up against what may be such a severe attack as to attempt to kill the analyst. At times, this is no mere psychological posturing, but is an extremely concrete attack, embodying the full force of hatred in the patient, to attempt to actually destroy the analyst and the analytic knowledge.

One day, Mrs B. had secretly brought a carving knife into the session and, acting with stealth but in a peculiarly obvious way that something was the matter, attempted to stab me to death—the voice demanded it. It is with interest that I can report that on the occasion that this happened, I had a sixth sense of some impending assault. In my countertransference, I felt a mixture of intense tiredness at the task and in addition an alertness to the minute details of my patient's physicality in the room. Even before the knife was made manifest from inside a towel where it was wrapped inside a large handbag, I had interpreted, following ten minutes of anxious painful silence, that there seemed to be a massive attack going on in the room and that it was causing her a great deal of anxiety. This led to the patient exposing the knife, saying that she wanted to plunge it into me as a way of appeasing the voices. I offered to look after the knife. Her relief was intense when she carefully and slowly held out the knife handle towards me, for me to look after. She was hugely grateful of the care given to her at being able to share her cruel hatred towards the other that also contained, fused together, her desire for revenge against her parents.

The capacity for differentiation between them and her analyst and the establishment of solid boundaries allowed her to know her wish to kill the analyst and also to know that he was also alive enough to the problem to be able to survive the assault. The nightly cutting of the body, as an attack on the self, was re-found in the transference, by Mrs B. attempting to put the knife into the analyst. Her body was his body, in the same dynamic way that his dog's shit was food for her mouth: an interpenetrating psychotic muddle, to paraphrase Balint, that in its understanding returns the vicious paranoia to a benign mutual understanding. Aggression against the self moves to the other. This enables the activity to be understood and interpreted, in time, both in the transference of the here and now and in reference to the past parental assaults. The difficult task of disentangling phantasy from reality needs to be attempted in the examination of the violence in the transference and countertransference. However, this can only really happen once the real threat of a real, sharp knife in the consulting room has been acknowledged and neutralized. Otherwise, the psychotic state of the patient may understand the not dealing with the weapon as a psychotic invitation by the analyst, issued through masochistic desire to be knife-penetrated as a way of being at one with the other.

The analyst must be extremely thorough in examining his own desire for revenge against such assault. Of course, the patient expects to be attacked back, as she feels she has been for most of her life by her primary objects. The patient may be constantly in a state of expecting that the treatment will just be stopped. This may take the opposite form of the patient trying to stop therapy in order to pre-empt her phantasy of the analyst's punishment of her coming true. Sometimes the patient's expectation of the analyst's desire for revenge (in identification with the patient) is an accurate reflection of the analyst not being able to stay further in the quagmire of the transference–countertransference. The patient's wish and expectation of being too much for anybody to cope with can then come true. The analyst may think that he has done enough in an impossible case, but this needs to be perhaps understood as a revenge motif, and instead perhaps the analyst can continue to do analysis with the patient. At this point, the analyst can make a clinical decision about whether the patient is unworkable with, as there is such a high risk of violence, primarily towards the analyst. Psychiatric care as an inpatient needs to be considered. However, if the home situation is amenable enough, analysis of the psychotic state (to include such violent fantasies with the analyst taking all necessary precautions in order to stay with the storm) can result in an analytic movement to a benign state in which interpretative work can be done about the preceding violent crisis.

The capacity of the analyst to bear such work is clearly connected with the analyst's own state of mind. Difficult or impossible patients may well be treatable by certain analysts, as long as they only have one such case currently in their practice. Working in analysis six sessions weekly then becomes an intense holding that converts the consulting room into the holding of the mental hospital that enables the patient to stay with the clinical material with the analyst. If the patient is returned to the mental hospital, their own unconscious aggressive phantasies will continue, but in the absence of the analyst, who may be understood as not able to bear it. The authenticity of who is doing what for whom is crucial at such moments. It is easy to say that the patient requires more or a different form of care, but if there is silence about how the violence impacts the analyst, the patient will often reverse such a thought projectively into the mind of the analyst, as if it originated in him. Again, as in the history, this will be experienced as being cruel, pushing her away and into an environment that is far from placid and benign—as anyone who has spent nights in a psychiatric unit can testify.

In the examination of countertransference phenomena, the horror of the knowledge can lead to the analyst accepting, as it were, the patient's own defence of being at a distance. The sense of becoming used to horror needs to be thought about so that despite being "battle-hardened", one is still able to feel. Consciously, Mrs B. strove to stay in the crack in the ceiling, looking down at the scene! This was an affectless position, in order to survive. Without doubt, the analyst also occupies such a space at times, with his own unconscious defensive structure available. So perhaps the actual assault on the boundaries of the analyst by bringing a knife into the frame is an unconscious attempt to get closer and to enable initially the analyst and later the patient to be in touch with the terrible affect of murder, murderous guilt, and then expiation. Such material is an ordinary part of the neurotic Oedipus complex. However, for the psychotic patient, it is experienced as a concrete thing. The real danger of an explosion of violence makes such work with a psychotic patient extremely difficult. It does not stay in the realm of the imaginary, but of action, and often dangerous action.

Paolo Uccello, Saint George and the Dragon. Bought with a special grant and other contributions, 1959 © The National Gallery, London.

In the fifteenth century, Paolo Ucello painted a mysterious picture of St George and the Dragon, which can now be found in the National Gallery, London. At a quick glance, it seems as if St George, on a white charger, is rushing to the rescue of the damsel menaced by a large green dragon. This scene takes place with a background of a rocky cave to the left and a forest with a cloudy swell like an eye on the other side of the picture behind the horseman. Yet, the damsel is not distressed. In fact, she is holding a lead attached to the dragon that is her pet. Such a picture provides a very vivid example of how the therapist needs to exercise great caution prior to rushing in to effect a rescue. The death of the maiden's pet animal is not something that is going to lead to a positive therapeutic experience or alliance. Killing the patient's protective dragon may not be accepted well initially. As a motif, it reflects the simplistic idea that the analyst will rescue the patient from their tormenting illness, even if, coming upon a woman and a dragon in the forest, it would be hard not to think about danger—for the maiden or oneself.

The noose around the dragon represents the seriousness of the symptoms that need to be respected, especially as, by reversal, it may be understood as the psychotic patient being tightly in the grip of the kept dragon monster. As a surface picture of the primal scene and the struggle between a damsel and a knight, one could think of the scene of the psychosexual work of a neurotic transference. Yet the dangerous presence of a fire-breathing dragon in the centre of the primal scene is indicative of work with psychosis. This psychotic functioning takes place in darker recesses—the darkness of the masochistic maternal cave and the paranoid paternal monitoring eye. In both states of mind, the actual trauma inflicted on the baby, the child, and the adolescent is a decisive factor in the structuring of the sexual state of mind.

One needs to see despite being blinded, and the patient's terrible task is to catch sight of that which was real and feel it rather than to constantly deny its existence whilst simultaneously repetitively manufacturing it in present times.

CHAPTER FIVE

Daydreams, dreams, and trauma

*When they were building the walls, how could I not have Noticed! But
I never heard the builders, not a sound. Imperceptibly they've closed me
off from the outside world.*

—C. V. Cavafy, *Walls* (1896, p. 3)

This paper will examine the damage that early trauma can inflict
on dream states. For some severely traumatized patients, there
can be an ongoing failure of dream work. The affect from both
the past and the present can fail to even be mobilized and, as such,
psychic energy is withdrawn from the dream machine. So the same
dream whirrs round again and again repetitively, but devoid of the possibility of a creative drive.

The repetitious nature of such dreams is often unnoticed by the
patient. The analyst may regard them as familiar yet flat and unyield-
ing to further knowledge or exploration, as if they contain a resistance
to dream interpretation itself. Attempting to understand and make connections beneath the surface structure of the repetitious manifest content
can lead to change in the patient. Identity organized around trauma but
with unconscious control exercised against any felt emotional life can

often be noticed in the countertransference. If changes can occur in the affect system of the patient, the emergence of closer contact with reality can result.

One year before his death in 1938, Freud wrote on understanding dreams:

> Every dream that is in process of formation makes a demand upon the ego—for the satisfaction of an instinct, if the dream originates from the id; for the solution of the conflict, the removal of a doubt or the forming of an intention if the dream originates from a residue of preconscious activity in waking life. The sleeping ego, however, is focused on the wish to maintain sleep. It feels this demand as a disturbance and seeks to get rid of the disturbance. The ego succeeds in doing this by what appears to be an act of compliance: It meets the demand with what is in the circumstances a harmless fulfilment of a wish and so gets rid of it.
>
> (Freud 1938, pp. 169–170)

Freud retained the idea that as a central theme, every dream is a disguised wish fulfilment, yet in addition he was interested in the use of dreams as a solution to unconscious conflict. The dream reproduces conflict between the dynamic agencies in the mind. The usefulness of the dream is to reveal unconscious desire, as a route into thinking, which has its correspondence in early memories and, concomitantly, in treatment, in representation in the transference.

The dream acts as a specific observation platform into the internal world. The dream is close to childhood memories as they both essentially use pictorial representation. The dream is more often than not visual, and most adult recollections of early childhood are also similarly known through pictures or scene. Associations in analysis often have in their core a small fragment of historical experience, which may lead to further memories and thoughts, and it is such fragments and details which may then be captured in the dream as part of the day residue. Often, a patient's response to either an accurate or a near-accurate interpretation is to dream a particular fragment that can help with understanding or providing confirmation of that analytic position. I do not mean dreaming to fit in with the analyst, but through the analyst and analysand dyad, together pushing the work forwards (or backwards). It is aspects of such fragments in dreams relating to trauma that I particularly want to examine.

In *Beyond the Pleasure Principle*, Freud described a class of dreams that are a serious exception to the rule that dreams are wish fulfilments: "They occur in patients suffering from accidents that also occur during the psychoanalysis of neurotics and bring back to them forgotten traumas of childhood" (Freud 1920, p. 5).

Expanding on Freud's theme of the repetition of traumatic experience as represented in the dream, Ferenczi wrote the following:

> It strikes us more and more that the so called days (and we may also add life's) residues are indeed repetition symptoms of traumata ... thus instead of the "dream as a wish fulfilment", a more complete definition of the dream function would be: every dream, even an unpleasurable one, is an attempt at a better mastery and settling of traumatic experiences ... [ ] ... which is made easier in most dreams because of the diminution of the critical faculty and the predominance of the pleasure principle.
>
> (Ferenczi 1931, p. 238).

If we follow Ferenczi's argument when treating severely traumatized patients who appear to have a paucity of affect, the dream can provide a core means of making sense of a deeply unconscious traumatic state of mind. At the same time, the dream is the mode through which a new creative direction can emerge if the analyst is able to connect it to movement in the transference and emotional life. In chronic repetitive dreams where the need to master appears so essential, the usual functions of dreaming, especially of dream affect, may be damaged, as is the function of wish fulfilment.

Winnicott described an incapacity to dream in *Playing and Reality*:

> Dreams fit into object relating in the real world and living in the real world fits into the dream world in ways that are quite familiar, especially to psychoanalysts. By contrast, however, fantasising remains an isolated phenomenon, absorbing energy but not contributing either to dreaming or to living. To some extent fantasising has remained static over the whole of this patient's life, that is to say dating from very early years, the pattern being established by

the time she was two or three. It was in evidence at an even earlier date and it probably started with a "cure" of thumb sucking.

(Winnicott 1971, p. 31)

Here, Winnicott is describing normal unconscious seamlessness between dream state and reality.

He continues:

> Another distinguishing feature between these two sets of phenomena is this, that whereas a great deal of dream and of feelings belonging to life are liable to be under repression, this is a different kind of thing from the inaccessibility of the fantasising. Inaccessibility of fantasising is associated with dissociation, rather than repression. Gradually as this patient begins to become a whole person and begins to lose her rigidly organised dissociations, so she becomes aware of the vital importance that fantasising has always had for her. At the same time the fantasising is changing into imagination related to dream and reality.

(ibid., p. 31)

Winnicott understands a trajectory from apparently not having daydreams to being able to imagine, and its effect on dreams and integration. This is in the same territory as Bollas's "unthought known" (Bollas 1987, p. 277) where a discovery is made that something is found that has the ring of always having been known, but unfound in one's mind until that moment of finding. The analysand has no idea about knowing something until it is able to be a thought in the conscious mind, where it can be welcomed, as a thought always to have been known, now that it has been located in consciousness.

The process of trauma and its attack on the mind can lead to a process of what Ferenczi first described as "atomization" (Ferenczi 1931, p. 234) that can affect psychopathology in several directions. For instance, let us return to Freud's observation in *Neurosis and Psychosis*, already discussed in Chapter One, that,

> we know that other forms of psychosis, the schizophrenias are inclined to end in affective hebetude—that is in a loss of all participation in the external world. In regard to the genesis of delusions, a fair number of analyses have taught us that the delusion

is found applied like a patch over the place where originally a rent had appeared in the ego's relation to the external world.

(Freud 1924, p. 151)

Affective hebetude does not mean that life is not being noticed. On the contrary, there is often a heightened state of noticing what is going on around, but it is done in such a way that it may be difficult to detect under the cover of mental fragmentation.

Such states of mind can lead to obsessive-compulsive disorders in which there is an emptying out of affect and disassociation from reality as a way of providing a particular type of unconscious mental balance. If there are particular states of excitation in relation to, say, sexuality, then the fragmentation of mind in relation to early trauma may well find expression in perverse phantasies that can lead to perverse enactments. It is likely that the particular perverse fault lines and structures come about in relation to the particular occurrence and type of trauma and its impact at particular developmental times of the genital organization and the Oedipus complex. Sometimes such sexual assaults, real, *après coup*, and imaginary, attacking the mind can lead to attacks on thinking that is the clinical picture of schizophrenia.

Disturbed patients who have been traumatically damaged can often be observed to have repetitious debilitating enactments in their daily lives without any apparent dreaming. It is likely that such states of mind, despite containing an attempt at some healing of the gap, include particular dream forms, probably along a continuum between incapacity to dream at one end to repetitious empty dreams at the other. Arguably along such a dream fault line is an attack on the actual dream mechanism itself, which may have become structurally damaged. Either no dream work is going on, or it occurs but is unknown consciously. However, it is also possible that dream work consists, in some psychotic states, of repetitious dreams devoid of affect but continually re-presented in a hollow way—a sort of "as if" dreaming state. Such "false" or damaged dreams are the equivalent of false selves.

Psychoanalytic treatment can then be thought of as a process that might be able to first restore a damaged repetitious dream from the "no dream" position. In time, it may then be able to connect dreaming with affect, which is more able to bear the emotional life, memory, history, and the pain of the transference, rather than a bland or enacted dismissal of all such emotional life.

I will now examine some clinical work within this theoretical framework. Firstly, I will examine daydreams and dreams across two consecutive sessions of a neurotic patient in analysis and, secondly, some material from a supervision session. Then I will also present some material from the analysis of a schizophrenic patient, Mrs B. (previously discussed in Chapter Four).

The following two sessions are from the third year of a five times weekly analysis of a young woman, Miss A. She grew up feeling herself to be alienated from her mother, who was pregnant with her prior to getting married. Feeling herself to have been an unwanted baby, she regarded her younger brother as having been more loved and cared for than she felt she had been. He was bought expensive birthday presents, cars, and expensive holidays, none of which had been offered to her. He seemed to be at the centre of family life whilst she felt ignored.

Session one

The first session after an Easter break

Miss A.: As I was leaving at the end of the last session, I realized I had a daydream.

"I met a two year old who had no parents, just at the top of the staircase. I thought of bringing her to you as she was crying. I wondered what you would think and I wondered how you would deal with it." It's me. [At that time, my consulting room was located in the basement of a house and was reached by a staircase going down from the pavement level.]

This was at once followed by her describing a dream she had had on Easter Sunday.

Miss A.: *"You followed me to my house, I was in my car and you did a Jesus impression. I had to get away. I had to be very careful of a wheelchair which had one wheel in the gutter."*

She associated that it made her think that one of her legs was longer than the other as she was growing up, "My mother's solution was that I should walk with one leg in the gutter." It was only at age fourteen that a doctor diagnosed a mild scoliosis when it was realized that one of her legs was actually a little longer than the other.

Analyst: Perhaps you feel I'm going to be like your mother—somebody to "get away" from?

Miss A.:   The two year old was bright, intelligent, and vivacious. There was nothing wrong with her.

When my father's mother died, I remember that she adored me, bought me things, a white coat, blue shoes. She didn't like my mother. She died of cancer in her late fifties.

Analyst: Perhaps she was a good parent that you thought you had lost.

Miss A.:   I thought she had seen me from heaven. She would see all the bad stuff and I was very preoccupied with this.

Analyst: Like in your dream, me being Jesus killed on Easter Sunday and in heaven seeing what you were up to over the Easter break.

Miss A.:   As a teenager I feared that I would have cancer.

Analyst: Perhaps the shock of losing your grandmother was very profound. In the dream, you conjure me up and you also fear and wish losing me.

Miss A.:   It was very difficult at Christmas, but I thought it was all right over Easter.

Analyst: In the daydream, there was an alive baby with no parents and in a way you've been like that in the dark, really alone for years.

Miss A.:   I have a memory of my father in the bathroom. I was watching him shave. He made a pretend razor for me. I was eight or nine. I felt close to him. When his father died, he went without my mother for the funeral. There was no sadness in the house, I felt confused and scared.

I was having some difficult thoughts about my sexuality, about not looking feminine. I saw a photograph of myself two years ago, my hair was in a bob. I was very upset.

Session two

The following day's session

Miss A.:   I'm mad. A senior colleague was teaching me. He's been having a threesome with my flatmate and her friend. His wife has just given birth. I asked him how it was before I knew of the threesome. He said his daughter had dirty blonde hair. I felt very upset and was very cross with my flatmate. I want to shout at her.

Analyst: It seems that you're morally upset. Maybe underneath this, you are cross about their sexual freedom. Yesterday you spoke of your uncertainty about being a boy or a girl, so we can think, "it's disgusting" with whatever you imagine went on, men with women, women with women.

Miss A.: You might be right. I hate my flat mate … my mother forgot to phone me on my birthday, she also didn't wish me well for my exams, although she did send a present.

Bodies are difficult. It's alright on the surface, not underneath. My mother would bath leaving the door open. My father sometimes walked around the house naked. I hated the moles on his back and his penis.

I looked in the mirror when I was eight or nine. It's difficult to say this, but I thought I saw I had a penis. I was very embarrassed. I am very embarrassed. I hate even using such words.

Analyst: Perhaps it was easier to ally yourself to father than mother. You began saying you were mad. Of course this can mean cross, or your fear that you would be (mad) like your mother, therefore better to be a boy (which is also mad in a different sort of way).

Miss A.: I told you I had vaginissmus at first.

Later in the session, in relation to previous material, I said:

Analyst: It's like you didn't dare discover that you didn't have a penis and you don't have a vagina—that it too is lost and needs to be found and it is not just somatic but a mental vaginissmus of not wanting to think, therefore, no penis, no vagina, no mind.

Miss A.: I better throw this in … as a kid I masturbated with the fantasy of being tied up. I suppose if I was passive I could not be blamed. I did it to ease the tension so I could sleep.

Analyst: Too much tension or not enough pleasure. You think masturbation is bad. You think you might be mad. I don't think you are, but your mind and body are lost to you and need to be found.

Miss A.:   Well I can do all that, but behind my professional self I hate it, as I have hated sex. My boyfriend and the other men; it is all disgusting.

At the beginning of the first session, a daydream comes to the mind of Miss A. with the following components. A two-year-old with no parents stood by an image of a staircase, inviting thoughts of sexuality (by this is meant the movement up and down) as well as being descriptive of her actual journey to reach the consulting room. Affect is implied with the mention of crying, and there was concern about what I might think about her.

Very quickly, there is a merging as well as an unravelling between the daydream and the night dream. Miss A. remembered the absence of parents and of her analyst during the break in treatment, which is the point of transference in which she feels alone and abandoned. Furthermore, with an early memory of eight or nine, there is a mixture of sexual ideas including her identification with her father, her imagining that she has a penis, and a perverse fantasy. The patient, not unnaturally, is uncertain whether any of this can be talked about, heard by me, or even understood. What is interesting is that in the dream she is beginning to be in touch with her polymorphously perverse young child self. An unconscious phantasy may have been developing that "boys are cared for, so I'll think of myself as a boy and father will protect me from mother and I'll unconsciously imagine that I have identified with him and even take his phallus for myself".

The Easter break brought with it a repetition of her being alone, without parents and in the absence of analysis. She unconsciously imagined that I had to get away from her damaging rage and then I would return with a vengeance to put her in a wheelchair. Such possibilities frightened her, leading to the element in the dream of me as Jesus, together with the wheelchair in the gutter, as if she fears that her hopes of salvation in analysis will only leave her in the gutter, as perhaps the break in analysis had left her. Yet this too is the start of another thread in her history of psychosomatics, as she had a problem of locomotion. She had been born with a lumbar scoliosis, which was undiagnosed until her early teens. Her mother always thought that her walking oddly and not keeping up with the rest of the family was wilful on her part. It took a school doctor to diagnose that there actually was a physical problem. Here again, we can meet the sense of unfairness and cruelty towards her from her mother, which may well have led her to believe her body was damaged, developing into an unconscious idea that her sexuality was also damaged.

In my mind, there is a question of whether she had had the thought that her mother had actually tried to abort her on hearing the news that of being pregnant out of wedlock. This is a scenario in which she might have unconsciously thought that she had been damaged from the start of her life—located in the gutter and got rid of. Miss A. felt that she had always to get away and stay emotionally alone as the powerful solution through which she attempted to solve her life. The patient is using both phantasy and dream imagery to allow access to her internal world. This is an example of an analysand needing to be brave to do this, as it reveals her acute sense of aloneness, the emotional neglect in her history, and the inadequate defensive responses required to cover up her hatred. After all, following the birth of Jesus at Christmas, he is cruelly killed at Easter, both evocations redolent of analytic breaks. Miss A.'s bravery extends to having a daydream just after leaving a session and being able to remember it in order to tell it at the beginning of the next session, despite it making her feel very vulnerable. This is because she is able to speak more openly about her wish to communicate, even though she has reservations about her mother's and her analyst's disinterest.

In the dream of the first session, she is able to dream about a direct wish to get away from me because it would enable her to more easily keep her defences intact. These are the same defences that enabled her, when her parents sent her away to boarding school, to feel that she was coping despite being an alone adolescent. Here is a dream state in which the enactment of her wishing to get away from the analyst is a reversal of a trauma of feeling that her parents had got away from her, with her being left, humiliated and alone in the gutter. By being able to dream this, there is an acknowledgement of the pain of the reality of being left out that she was beginning to be able to face in the transference—being left in the Easter break.

In addition is the knowledge that the small child in the daydream wanted me to know what was happening, so that the dream wish was that she might be cared for and that the traumatic moment might be contained. In this example, the trauma is about absence, as in not being noticed or not feeling cared about. (Other types of trauma will include too much intrusion into mind or body, which is an opposite of absence.) The daydream and dream interplay together to enable her to unconsciously activate the parental transference, as well as the possibility of a new beginning in which she could be noticed, heard, and could begin to share her feelings with another person. This is a most unusual turn for a person who keeps her thoughts and feelings almost totally to herself. The trauma finds expression through daydreams and dreams into the transference where it can be made known and externally connected with the analyst. In this example, the daydream and night dream are able to function and develop each with the other in expanding the knowledge of a traumatic history and dealing with the vicissitudes of ordinary daily life. The analyst who disappears in the holiday needs to be considered as a further example in present times of an earlier uncaring, even murderous, object. The analytic work then is to examine her child wish for a penis, revealed as a hallucination, as a particular somatic patch on her body that is intended to protect her from the imagery of being unwanted. The somatic hallucination identifies her as a boy, like her well-loved brother.

Supervision session

This material is from the therapy of a female patient who was herself a trainee therapist working in another country. The patient had an ambiguous sexuality and was described as being competitive with her own therapist. At the time, treatment was twice a week and there had been discussion of a third session. Supervision was weekly.

The therapist had cancelled a previous week of sessions for a holiday. At the next session, when the patient arrived, she found the toilet was occupied. Hearing noise, the therapist came out of her consulting room and felt obliged to explain to her patient that an old lady from the other office might be using the toilet. The patient, who always went to the toilet prior to the session, replied that it did not matter. The therapist thought there was no clinical material to look at as her patient travelled far to get to her, necessitating an apparently natural requirement for the toilet.

After a while, the patient complained of a headache that she had had over the last few days and this led to the remembering of a dream.

Dream One: "Someone is in my bedroom and is assaulting me."

The patient had had thousands of daydreams of being assaulted. It was a device to put herself to sleep at night. She had feelings that she was getting out of the room, or never getting out of the room. It was not her fault, she said, that the ultimate fantasy was suicide, as well as imagining how others might respond when one is dead. There was a feeling of annihilation as everything felt *"in a million pieces"*. The patient seemed to be speaking of her fixed beating fantasy. Curiously, she described in her associations Ferenczi's idea of atomization after the aggressive idea of death by suicide.

The patient said she had stayed grounded the previous week when her therapist was away: *"I was not a frightened bird but grounded in the present."*

Therapist: Yet you had a fight in your head—headaches for those days.

"Yes it makes me think of rage and violence. My words disappear in a void (heard as avoid). I have to get really close to a person to miss them. My thoughts are fragmented. I felt I smelt my cousin at the beginning of the session, ready to take a beating. When we were young, my cousin and I were cruel to a friend. When she was in the toilet we broke in and tormented her."

Now let us look at the material in light of some earlier experiences of this patient. For many years when growing up, she apparently had sexual explorations, leading to intercourse with her brother who was three years older than her. Any feeling of being cared for invariably led this patient to imagine his beautiful face. She felt he loved her and she loved being in his arms. There is a split in her mind as she remembered being woken up abruptly and harshly by him in the night and being fondled. When eventually she told her mother about what had been happening, she was invited to pray and only that. In the history, there is a story that her mother had herself been assaulted as a child.

One can think of this material as a chronic attack on a little girl who had vacuous and unboundaried parents. A split then developed in her mind that eulogizes the love of the brother, raises that relationship on to a pedestal, and erotizes her anxiety. All this covered over the profound destructive emptiness and the assault on her body and mind during her development. Mental development becomes structured around a fixed, repetitive daydream of assault—somebody entering a room to attack, somebody receiving an attack, which becomes defensively both erotic and exciting. Again, the material chimes with Freud's "A Child is Being Beaten" which was examined in the previous chapter. In the daydream, she is in charge and no longer the victim. Perhaps this is an easier mental state to bear, despite its perversity, than her having to notice feelings of suicidal despair from the absence of her desire for loving, caring parents. This cruelty becomes the unconscious desired enactment in the transference.

In the material of the reported session, we hear that when young, the patient broke into a toilet to torment a friend. We learn that she went to the toilet prior to the start of every session. The therapist, unaware of the beating daydream structure as an enactment at the start of each session, is rooted in what Ernest Jones called "rationalization" (Jones 1951, p. 225). The therapist is concerned that as the patient travelled a long way to reach each session, she would, of course, require a toilet visit preceding each session. Perhaps the unconscious punishment for a cruel unconscious phantasy towards the therapist is the gap between each session, mitigated by the patient placing herself in the receiving position of being in the toilet awaiting the "assault" from her therapist as a kind of talion. It is likely to also include its opposite—that she enters the toilet as a representation of her therapist who she feels is then vulnerable to the patient's wish to beat her. Such unconscious ideas may well be compounded by the week's enforced break by the therapist.

To recap, the following lines appear in the material: a dream of the patient being assaulted in her bedroom and a daydream of her being assaulted. The patient remembered as a child a cruel torment that she perpetrated on a friend who was invaded upon when on the toilet. She remembered having a sexual relationship with an older brother, in the light of a very indifferent mother. The transference just prior to each session of the patient's enactment of a "toilet scene" was an important enactment. There is a dream-like quality connecting things and happenings. In particular, what draws attention to a seemingly ordinary moment, just prior to the session, is that the toilet is engaged, inviting the patient to remember her role, when a child, of forcing entry. This is a complex medley of dream, daydream, remembrance, and whatever the status of the truth of the matter, there is a description of an assault on a child. All the facets are potentially available to be viewed in the transference. It is much more complex than just a surface description of the gap between sessions since the weekend.

A seemingly innocent beginning needed to be grasped by the therapist, and then the different strata of trauma can be examined. The patient felt prevented from entering the toilet, as was her habit. The not being allowed is in opposition to earlier traumas of doing to and having done to her, in relation to her brother. Despite her own early sexual history, her mother's reaction of inviting only prayers was profoundly unhelpful. Essentially, her mother is unconsciously saying to her daughter—you and I are the same, we were both sexually abused, and now all we can do is pray.

The traumatic fragments are in both the daydream and the dream and can be emotionally re-found in transference and countertransference in the consulting room. How interesting that the therapist felt obliged to go outside her door to find out about a commotion, as well as needing to let her patient know that the toilet was occupied. Perhaps this is an example of a countertransference enactment of intervening at some happening, rather than accepting the usual way—like, perhaps, mother who just accepted whatever her son and daughter might have been doing and did not open the door to an intervention. The problem is that the therapist's explanation to the patient about the use of the toilet by an old lady is outside the session and analytically detached; although it would be accurate to observe it as a countertransference enactment of much interest.

Understanding the therapist's intervention may herald a deepening of emotionality, as a means of bringing a well-told repetitive story into an alive transferential position. Then the affect, so far hidden, can be re-experienced. The patient revealed her unconscious sadomasochism around a closed door that must be opened, that can be regarded as a defensive structure in which the traumatic assault on a small girl is confused with identification with the aggressor. Beneath this structure is likely to be the misery of a small child lost, damaged, and alone. This describes a particular type of trauma on a continuum from aloneness to over-intrusiveness into the mind and/or the body. The direction of therapy is to locate the original traumatic position. As the dream states, "I am in my bedroom and somebody is assaulting me." There is no affect in the telling of this dream. In fact, it is a dream that is dreamt repetitively and chronically with any emotionally attached experience leached away. There is no escape, and the direction is only one of mastery to enjoy the repetition, identify with the aggressor, and turn what needs to be a dream experience into a nothing (no thing) experience. For the patient, it is just another boring repetition of unhelpful sameness and holds no particular interest.

Six months later, the therapist took another break from the treatment, and it is interesting to observe the dream material in the first session back at work. The patient commenced by describing two dreams. In the first dream, she was on holiday with an old lady of around fifty or sixty years of age: "She and I were interchangeable. We had sores all over our bodies. Yet we had the choice of location. So I kept them off my face so nobody would know."

> Dream Two: "Just at the start of the holiday, I dreamt someone was breaking into my bedroom."

The patient was now able to notice that the old lady represented her perceived "old" therapist as well as her mother. This is in line with a brief report of an young physician writing to Freud about having a religious conversion following seeing "a sweet old woman who was being carried to a dissecting-table" (*A Religious Experience*, p. 169). The new judgement in that report about religion followed a renewal of an unconscious Oedipal tussle. Of course, there had been the previous old lady that the therapist had remarked on being in the toilet, without noticing the element of potential transference. Now she was able to begin to recognize how she interchanged such representations. This seemed an important crux of her stuckness because there was no need to move positions if one could, whimsically, be the other. She had no curiosity about being in such a replication of the self. Her mother's lack of concern when her daughter bravely told her of the sexual happenings with the brother is changed into mother having had the same done to her. It is as if her mother was saying "as I have had this done to me as well, therefore we are interchangeable". This structure was then developed and enacted in the transference with the trainee therapist analysand, in treatment with the trained therapist and in perceiving no difference between the two. Interchangeability is a massive defensive structure that enabled the patient to identify with the aggressor, brother, mother, lover, and therapist without the reverberations of affect. Yet this dream is juxtaposed in the telling next to the old repetitive affectless dream of "someone is breaking into my bedroom". One might notice a development in the structure of dreaming—the old position, of a break-in, at the start of the break in therapy, is brought into use in order to not make any difference. This leads to a neutralization by being back in the same old defensive position. The first told dream, perhaps dreamt after the second one and just prior to the start of the term, is full of movement rather than stuckness. The idea of the "sore" being hidden away from the face, yet concealed on the body, is a motif that showed that, beneath the surface of visibility, there were many sore areas. Now such sore areas did not need to be concealed so much, as they had representation in the dream. There was also a move away from a fixed position as there was a choice of location in the dream.

Speculatively, a movement from an empty dream to a full dream was the product of six months' solid therapeutic work. Associations full of affect spoken between the therapist and patient have been able to be taken into dream life as an antidote to the stuck affectless repetitious dream. There is now a possibility of a creative direction, with the emotional life of the patient now, at least, revealed as sores. In *The Interpretation of Dreams*, Freud used the term "daydream" synonymously with "phantasy" or "daytime phantasy", and these did not always need to be conscious: "there are unconscious ones in great numbers which have to remain unconscious on account of their content and of their origin from repressed material" (Freud 1900, p. 492).

Clinically, patients who found themselves left alone by adults for considerable periods during their early upbringing are likely to have well-developed defensive unconscious structures that often consist of a life filled with daydreams to fill up empty emotional space. The daydream can function as a kind of transitional holding of and by the self—like a transitional blanket. It is as if there is an emotional dialogue with the other when actually it is a statement of aloneness and emptiness.

To return to Miss A., she also presented much of the time in states of silence. This was not just in her analysis but in social settings. The silence expressed her deep humiliation as well as anxiety and embarrassment at being in the presence of anyone else, particularly in communications with other people. She was the silent person in the group, invariably uncertain of having anything to say in case it was wrong or stupid. She would consciously re-enact the biting sarcasm of her parents towards how useless she felt they experienced her. Contempt was already in her mind as an expectation of a defensive requirement as well as in identification with her mother. However, the long periods of silence gradually revealed a huge tendency towards daydreaming. These defences were only revealed with much hesitation, as in the transference she felt humiliated and on show to me, with an expectation of being hurt for having had such thoughts. (Later, in Chapter Seven, on "somatic resistance", we will return to her silence.)

The idea that in her silent daydreams she was constructing a web of "as if" relationships full of hopes and wishes was something hard for her to comprehend. The uppermost thought in her mind was how dangerous it was to reveal her emotional life to another person. Gradually, she realized that she actually did have plenty in her mind to think about, even to say. Miss A. was not the empty vacuous character that she presented herself as being. However, such a new set of ideas meant that, probably for the first time, she had to have a very different emotional relationship with another person, her analyst.

In time, she realized that the lives she had had with boyfriends were silent happenings. She did not mind having a sexual life with a man, as long as she did not have to participate emotionally. Her body was dissociated, and in her mind she could continue her daydreaming monologue alone and by herself. Through analysis, her one-person psychology was changing into two-person psychology. It was by her revealing her daydream life that she could begin to speak of her night dream life.

* * *

The schizophrenic patient Mrs B. spoke about her fear of horror movies and this led her to associations about beginning to daydream. This woman had described being brought up by cruel, persecutory parents who seemed to have very little concern for their daughter, but similar to the clinical vignette of Miss A., there was, at times, a doted-upon younger brother. With much humiliation, Mrs B. spoke of a persistent daydream that her tongue was being cut with a knife. She believed it connected with a similar thought that she might cut her tongue by licking the lid of a yoghurt pot, an activity she often did. She thought that this represented her greed and that her guilt at eating in that way necessitated punishment.

Mrs B. was able to continue to free associate to the daydream and reluctantly remembered with a great deal of horror many daydreams she had had of licking dog faeces from pavements. In fact, she could hardly bear to notice dog faeces around, and then realized she was always constantly on the look-out for them. Even more horrid was her thought that she would notice a runny mess. She knew this was different from human excreta including her own. Following her associations, she remembered an early memory before she was five years old. She had been out with her father and had fallen in some dog faeces and it had smeared her coat. He was not cross and, to her surprise, when she remembered, he had been quite kind. He took her home and cleaned her and her coat. In many years of analysis, this was the only time that she had ever mentioned her father doing anything that could be considered kind. She always spoke of his cruel torment and hatred for her. I interpreted that what she hated was a moment of father's kindness that she perhaps never felt she had again, and her pain was of losing that moment of being with kind father again.

Here, the daydream reveals an unusual moment of connectedness and the concern from her father residing unconsciously beneath the surface. It is repressed and subsequently covered over in the daydream by an anal thought of devouring faeces and a consequential conscious refusal to ever look at a horror movie. A reversal is set up in the patient's mind as a device to sequestrate the emotional kind and warm fragment that she has never been able to rediscover in relation to her father. Perhaps this is an example of Winnicott's idea of the "blacking over" of a picture by a child. That underneath the surface of what looks like only black emptiness there is a more vivid picture.

As Winnicott described:

> Hallucinating is pathological because of a compulsive element which can be explained in the following way. Something has been dehallucinated and in a secondary way the patient hallucinates in denial of the dehallucination. It is complex because first of all there was something seen, then something dehallucinated and then a long series of hallucinations, so to speak, filling the hole produced by the scotomisation.
>
> (Winnicott 1957, p. 41)

My patient's concern with horror movies covered over something else. It led to a daydream that covered the gap produced by the wiping out of the good memory of father, as it was too painful to remember in relation to the rest of her experience of him. Repeated emotional traumatic attacks on the little girl by her usually overbearing, contemptuous, and arrogant parents have left their mark with the over-arching symptom of a fear of "horror films" which must never be seen. The patient was anally fixated, fearing the introjection of what she might see on the pavement, and this had generally been known about in her analysis through repetition compulsion in her life and her obsessive personality. Her fixation also expressed the direction of her wish to sadistically retain and control her object.

Interested in the shock of trauma in Freud's own thinking, Jonathan Lear writes:

> he comes to realise that the pleasure principle and its variant the reality principle describe the mind only in, as it were, its normal pathological functioning. In traumatic neurosis, Freud sees that there are more serious pathologies that attack the mind directly. And he realises that the mind's attempt to heal itself—to restore functioning according to the pleasure principle—cannot itself be described in terms of the pleasure principle.
>
> (Lear 2000, p. 72)

For Freud, "these dreams are endeavouring to master the stimulus retrospectively, by developing the anxiety whose omission was the cause of the traumatic neurosis" (Freud 1920, p. 32). Repetitive dreams of traumatic neurosis are successive failed attempts to instil the capacity to dream in an ordinary, wish-fulfilling way.

For most patients, the meaning of repetition in dreams is a reminder that more analytic work is required to be done. However, for those patients who have been on the receiving end of enormous mental and physical assault, often from a very young age, the constancy of attack can fragment and "atomize" the mind (Ferenczi 1933, p. 165). Some patients have even felt that they experienced being hated when in the womb. "TZ speaks incessantly of hate waves which she had always felt as coming from her mother, according to her fantasy even when still in mother's womb" (Ferenczi 1930, p. 227). This can be felt as a sense of deadly emanations coming towards the patient from somewhere or someone. It is a particular variation of *après coup* where the subsequent phantasy is repositioned to an earlier time line, especially the thought "was I ever wanted?". The repetitions of some traumatic dreams in attempting to process such horror can be seen as fixed and without meaning. In such patients, an attempt to heal the fragmented unconscious mind by dreaming can fail to provide meaning. The repetition in the dream begins to succeed by bringing dream elements together to initiate a dream with some content, but the strands of the content are unable to knit together as an ordinary formed unconscious dream thought. So the repetitive dream fails in its task and becomes an empty meaningless proposition. As Lear points out, the compulsion to repeat, rather than containing a meaning, is redolent of failed meaning.

As Lear further argues,

> the insight that Freud opened up but could not really grasp is that some mental activity occurs without a purpose. Freud cannot see this because of all this thinking and research is directed towards finding hidden and deeper purposes. The repetition is not of content, but activity—the activity of self-disruption. Such disruptiveness in no way 'tends' towards restoration—it tends just as much towards the new mental creations. In fact it tends in no direction at all.
>
> (Lear 2000, pp. 80–81)

This direction leads Freud to postulate the death drive—so the point of all life is death, which Lear describes as a teleological principle. For Lear, Freud "is enacting the traumatic theory in his own construction of a theory of trauma" (ibid., p. 85) by postulating the death drive. The mind's disruption is contained by Freud and given a meaning by calling it "death". However, this is just a name to cover over the gap—the same gap described so eloquently by Freud in *Neurosis and Psychosis*. This is a radical thought. Analysts are constantly looking for and expecting to find unconscious meaning in the clinical encounter. We are confronted with an idea that is about the finding of the "no meaning" that the repetition can express. It is only by being in such a paradox, and realizing the nothingness that is being expressed by the patient, that something new may emerge. Perhaps there need be less concern about repetition compulsion as a symptom of the death drive, than about the epistemic function of this repetition. Yet, as Bollas notices (personal communication), even though Freud writes that "it is impossible to classify as wish-fulfilments the dreams we have been discussing which occur in traumatic neuroses" and other examples, within a few sentences he rediscovers a link between wishing and the unwished-for. Such dreams "arise, rather in obedience to the compulsion to repeat, though it is true that in analysis that compulsion is supported by the wish to conjure up what has been forgotten and repressed" (Freud 1920, p. 33). Bollas argues that the wish is not to have that particular dream, but to subject the trauma to the dream process itself, which will bind the anxieties still residing in the trauma. It will then become more possible to know and feel "anxieties whose omission was the cause of the traumatic neurosis" (ibid., p. 33).

Postulating the no-meaning state of the traumatic dream can itself function as a fulcrum for the possibility of change by allowing the return of the omitted anxiety. For this, there needs to be an analysis with a possibility of the traumatic no-meaning becoming a place for the beginnings of the possibility of play. Not "alone play", as a type of adult-distorted *Fort-Da* game, but instead play created by two persons, the analysand–analyst dyad. Here lies the possibility of the creative development of affect in the couple, then and now, that can be the road to providing meaning, *après coup*, to the meaningless dream. This has probably less to do, at times, with a succinct interpretation than a mood state that, for a moment, veers away from the paranoid channel that the traumatic material invariably runs in.

The function of wish fulfilment can be understood as a means rather than an independent aim. Ferenczi, in a note "On the Revision of the Interpretation of Dreams" (Ferenczi 1931, p. 238), describes separate levels of dreaming. A patient he had seen for many years recounted two or several dreams from each night. The first, experienced in the hours of the deepest sleep, was devoid of psychic content but left behind vague recollections of both physical and mental pain. A second period of dreaming resulted in memories of very vivid images—distortions and attenuations of the events of the first dream. The same occurrences, it seemed, were experienced in different ways in different layers of unconsciousness:

> Gradually it became clear that the patient could and must repeat the traumatic events of her life, purely emotionally and without any ideational contents, only in a deep unconscious, almost coma-tose sleep; in the subsequent less deep sleep, however, she could bear only wish-fulfilling attenuations.

> (Ferenczi 1931, p. 239)

Dreaming may have different possibilities of affect and elaboration with deep sleep, allowing connection with the re-experiencing of traumatic elements, whereas wish fulfilment may occur in periods of lighter sleep. The patient described woke up after the first, painful dreams; presumably, the overwhelming experience was interrupted, and in the second period of sleep, the dream images were variations of the first theme, only now they were distorted so as to be less painful or unpleasurable. "The first dream", Ferenczi sums up, "is purely repetition; the second an attempt at settling it somehow by oneself [...] Under the condition of an optimistic counterfeit the trauma may be admitted to consciousness" (ibid., pp. 240–241). This is a description of different dream states allowing the dreamer to be in touch with that which is bearable.

The repetitious "nondream" dream now makes sense as the pain barrier is still too high to permit content and affect. The dream repetition is an attempt to deal with the effects of traumatic shock on perception.

> An unexpected, unprepared for, overwhelming shock acts like, as it were, an anaesthetic ... by inhibiting every kind of mental activity and thereby provoking a state of complete passivity devoid of any resistance.
>
> (ibid., p. 239)

Ferenczi then describes how to deal with a clinical situation in which a core complex of the patient's life experience is impossible to reach:

> (1) The course of sensory paralysis becomes and remains permanently interrupted; (2) while the sensory paralysis lasts every mechanical and mental impression is taken up without any resistance; (3) no memory traces of such impressions remain, even in the unconscious, and thus the causes of trauma cannot be recalled from memory traces. If in spite of it, one wants to reach them, which logically appears to be almost impossible, then one must repeat the trauma itself and under more favourable conditions one must bring it for the first time to perception and to motor discharge.
>
> (ibid., p. 240)

In the repetition of the trauma in the dream material, the traumatic incident is not being perceived (or glimpsed) for the second time but for the first time, when it was in the real experience of mental and or physical assault. These original moments were recorded, but paradoxically not experienced. Something was impressed upon the one who was there at the time of the occurrence, but not on the "I", so that it left behind a trace. That trace becomes ego-alien and is the reason for the patient's resistance to the possibility of meaning and affect as it is felt to be "not-I". This seemingly logically confused description can be seen to presuppose the notion of splitting. If not even unconscious memory traces of the event remains, the part of the person that recorded the event must have been split off and made alien, thus being phenomeno-logically regarded "somewhere else" and not accessible to perception in a normal waking state.

Lear (2010), in reviewing Bollas's books *The Evocative Object World* and *The Infinite Question*, takes issue about every dream being a wish fulfilment. Bollas, on the other hand, cites Freud as having never let go of that concept, holding on to the hope that even if the dream wish could not be understood now, that it would be understood in the future. They are describing different levels or registers of the mind. Ferenczi provides the linking argument that transcription of an experience is split off, leaving empty dream terrains devoid of everything, includ-ing wishes. This is a continuing reaction to mental assault, and is sepa-rate from the dream functioning of the wish, which can escape from the repression to be able to be evoked and shaped in the dream in a lighter register of sleep.

Freud theorized the concept of splitting only as late as 1938, but descriptions of similar phenomena had occurred from early on in his writings. Not knowing whether the phenomenon is "something long familiar and obvious or [...] entirely new and puzzling" (Freud 1938, p. 275) describes the reaction of reasoning a conflict "with two contrary reactions" that of simultaneously recognizing and refusing to acknowl-edge reality—a solution which is paid for by a "rift in the ego" which fails to heal (ibid., pp. 275–276). Ferenczi's main contribution on this point lay in his emphasis on the connection between splitting and trauma, describing how the reaction of partial withdrawal from reality in splitting off a part of the ego resulted from "Each experience of terror thus implies this kind of splitting off" (Ferenczi 1932, p. 18); in other words, the reaction represents an adaptation to an unbearably painful and unresponsive environment and this adjustment comes at the cost of a partial loss of reality.

Ferenczi became convinced from his clinical practice that so many of his patients were unconsciously trapped in earlier mental states that were the result of severe trauma together with a defensive system that ambivalently wanted to be in touch with this experience, whilst simul-taneously recognizing that it became too painful in its constant repeti-tion. This chapter provides material from dreams and daydreams in the context of transference to understand and find pathways to rediscover lost affect. The empty repetition of the affectless dream is a means of psychically hanging on to the fragments which must not be evoked except in the shadows of their absence, and which in some manner honours a psychic atomization of early life. Such fragments have coalesced in a way that manages to hold the patient's unconscious life together. It probably helps to prevent a further mental slide into the much greater chaotic illness of frank paranoia and schizophrenia.

So much for the mastery function of the repetition. The usefulness of re-finding the trauma from dreams and its psychic development to transference means the possibility that the lost awful traumatic affect can be re-found in the presence of the analyst within the ordinary context of the daily session. It is the ability of such technique to reach through empty terrain that enables the lost, lonely, traumatized child in the adult to be re-found.

CHAPTER SIX

Psychosomatics and technique

It is generally well known that out of the crews of Whaling vessels few ever return in the ships on board of which they departed.

—Theodore Foster, *A Cruise in a Whale Boat, and Adventures in the Pacific Ocean* (1979, p. xv)

At the age of eight, the writer Aharon Appelfeld witnessed the pogrom in his hometown of Czernowitz. He saw the murder of his mother and, separated from the rest of family, survived by scavenging in the forests. Remembrance was complicated, he thought, by his having been too young a child to process much of what he saw. The past remains entirely physical for him: "etched inside my body but not in my memory" (Appelfeld 2005). More than half a century later, his feet still cause tension in his legs and this pain instantly transfers him back to his years in hiding. The very act of sitting or standing can conjure up hellish visions of packed railway stations; rotting straw or the call of a bird trigger visceral memories deep within his body.

The capacity for free association is both protected and inhibited by the movement of affect into the body, which acts as a container and can deflect away from the mind with its complexity of thoughts and associative strands. A particular part of the body with its physicality, such as a feeling of body rigidity or a certain sequence of movements, can contain that which must not be felt and integrated in the mind.

Appelfeld conveys a view of mental states that are extreme and alarming. At some time, he saw, heard, and felt, leaving him as the victim in a state of uncomprehending terror—responding perhaps with immobility, by being struck dumb, and by fleeing the scene to survive. This is descriptive of overwhelming trauma, even more so for a child, who had not yet developed sufficient mental capacity to process such awful events, although what adult has! Yet the mind needs protection from the impact of massive affect: a move from psyche to soma ensues. The body can take over in providing the contours of associations, but these are detached from a capacity to free associate. Thus, one finds a patient who adopts particular positions on the couch, a certain rigidity of limbs or never moving, as a means of concealing earlier trauma, far distant from some terrible knowing. Of course, there may be free associations but only up to a point, after which one can notice the inhibition in the body. This acts both to conceal and reveal. Such positional structures need to be noticed to allow for the possibility of movement away from stuckness and towards mental curiosity. Finding the words moves psychic energy from the thing (body) presentation to word presentation that enables affect to move from an attachment to the body to that of the clinical dyad. As with the rest of an analysis, this requires time to work through the newfound memories in terms of past relationships. The patient in his psychosomatic state is alone and does not expect, nor necessarily wish for, the intervention of the other. The unconscious expectation is that the other is not there to help, and often historically this has truth, as adults have not protected the infant from trauma and may even have caused it.

There is a new possibility in the telling, that the listener who may be benign can hear the patient, invariably for the first time. The move from soma to psyche critically contains a new beginning. This, under the everyday surface noise of the analysand, may be an unexpected and new position. The patient may know that the other is listening to them for the first time.

Clinical material

Here we meet again Miss A., a young woman, in five-times-weekly analysis for several years, who suffered the consequences of being unwanted during and after her mother's pregnancy, especially through her adolescence and being sent away. Much understanding had been excavated over time about her early life, the sense of abandonment, and its impact on her self and her relationships. In particular, there was evidence of a constant maternal paranoia always supported by her father. At times either of great stress or when life was moving along quite smoothly, there would be a return to her physical symptom of retching. Usually, this would be when Miss A. was imagining a good evening, a lovely meal, and becoming closer to her boyfriend, or similarly on the point of attaining some achievement at work. Then the symptom would return, leaving her fearful that her fantasy would actually happen, leaving her in need of a toilet where she could be alone in order to vomit. Subsequently, such a cycle would leave her feeling relieved in her body but terrible in her mind. Clearly, someone or something was making the patient feel sick such that it needed to be got rid of.

A session prior to the end of a term:

Miss A. began by saying that she had not wanted to leave the session yesterday but could not say it. She tried to keep her thoughts sterile. She had other thoughts but must not think them. She wondered if my wife breast-fed. Her mother hated the idea and did not do it, as she could not bear the mess. Everything had to be kept clean and sterile. I said that as long as there are no free associations here, with the implication they might be dirty, she kept her mother content in her mind. She thought this was true and knew such associations were good for her. She added that she both missed and hated me for being away when she would be on her own. Yet it was far more important that she wanted to know and think about the interpretations that I made about the forthcoming break but all "seemed sterile". She felt as if she was her "mother picking away at the argument". I interpreted the danger in the break as meaning that mother and she would argue in her mind, putting our work, and me, down. She said, "When you are away I call you horrible things ... Johnny." I said that Johnny was slang for a contraceptive as well as a play on my name and that she was using it to keep herself sterile from dirty analytic thoughts. She said that she knew I would say that and realized that she used the word "anal" as an abbreviation in her diary to note sessions. Yesterday, she felt better as talking beyond the sterile helped as she was so relieved to break through the barrier.

Concrete metaphors, utilizing a contraceptive cover to separate dirty words and dirty thoughts, imprison the patient and keep her alone. This cover was a mental barrier to the free flow of unconscious and conscious mental life across the divide to the other. The mother was disdainful of intimacy and desired the utmost cleanliness. The symptom of retching was what the wretch did as a means of messing up the purity. Vomiting was a symptom that attempts to break through the contraceptive barrier, although it is hard for the patient to acknowledge the metaphor as a sign for a need for a healthy messing up as a way of breaking through the sterility. It was likely that the symptom also contained the patient's unconscious idea that she was not wanted as a baby as if she was enacting a pregnant mother vomiting her. Indeed, she had had thoughts that her mother tried to abort her. So the symptom of vomiting contained the idea of the woman pregnant and rejecting. It is possible to label such a mental state as bulimic yet the dynamic complexity requires being elucidated.

After that piece of work, the patient was able to be more successful in her professional life and began living with her boyfriend. The symptom was not in evidence, although it still lurked in the shadow of her life. How had such a symptom been relegated from a constant presence? Free associations broke through the "Johnny" and were allowed to contaminate the sterility between analyst and analysand. The welcoming of the mess of the dirty thought in the analytic situation made redundant the necessity for warding it off into a sterile or vomiting-anal world. A movement from a primitive mouth-anus bowel led unconscious emotional life towards an ego more able to bear and enjoy the mess of ordinary human relationships.

Another female patient, Miss F., was born to a young mother of fifteen. Her teenage mother had probably used the baby as a protective device from a much older husband and adult world—as something to cling onto. Over time, the mother had become more paranoid, not desiring her daughter to grow up and separate from her. Later, she tried to follow her daughter to university in another city and then had phoned incessantly trying to visit many times a week. This terrorism against the daughter led to the development, in Ferenczi's term, of a "wise baby", who from early on attempted to mother her mother, as she knew she was incapable of much adult functioning. Since being in analysis, the patient was able to put up a much greater barrier to her mother's huge intrusiveness. Instead of being in an oppositional state to mother's desired control, the patient has been more thoughtful and creative in the development of her own life. It was a hard-won realization that opposing her mother's encroachments had led to her living a kind of "oppositional life". This was different from the possibilities of an alternative life not tied to her intense unconscious defensiveness, leaving her far from free to live her life despite knowing about the maternal shadow.

Yet there was a subtle somatic symptom. Despite being very keen on analysis (attending five times a week, making much use of the work, and thinking it had saved her life), the patient lay nearly totally rigid on the couch. It was rare for her to move during the fifty minutes. Despite making intellectual strides, it points to a psychosomatic expression of her great unconscious anxiety, "I had better not move a muscle because mother will see and want to envelop me further" and/or "If I do not move I will stay hidden from her".

The patient had been able to question her capacity to appear to get what she wants in life. In job interviews and amongst colleagues, she seemed to charm others to her ideas. Indeed, she was able to develop an intelligence that allowed her to better organize her world but with the unconscious expectation always that the metaphor of the mother returning to possess her was always just a movement away. To the onlooker, the patient would appear much improved, perhaps nearing the end of a good analysis. Yet the shadow of the mother had been skilfully suppressed from view, becoming visible in the psychosomatics of the patient lying on the couch unmoving. There was more work to do.

A middle-aged homosexual man, Mr D., came to analysis because he had a failing relationship with an exceedingly demanding and much younger lover. It was soon apparent that he lived his intimate relationships in a sadomasochistic bind. He was failing in his work and was enraged at how he was unable to speak up to colleagues and at meetings despite realizing that he had good things to say. He was describing a reluctance really to engage with his life.

In time in the analysis, he moved from the telling of the facts of his life, to realizing that he had not spoken about sex. He began to dare to talk of the constant need to have poor, younger, out of work foreign partners. Ostensibly, he was the older and richer house owner who could be father to the younger men. He went further and revealed his massive anxiety about the moment of bodily intimacy when both partners became naked. His life was fixed at avoiding this in all manner of ways. He feared that his penis was too small. Always the imagining was that the fitter young men were larger and he could only balance the bodily discrepancy by being the older richer man able to look after "the young cock".

This was a revelation, and to his surprise he did not feel humiliated. The expected dyad of one big person and one small person did not appear in the clinical setting. Instead, his free association was in the spirit of the equality of dialogue between analyst and analysand. This was a very different resonance to the usual sadomasochistic expectation of his fixed relationships. Over the next few months, with firm kindness he got rid of the younger man, who he now realized was a somewhat nasty and demanding cuckoo in his nest. He found he could speak more freely at work, realized he was listened to, and achieved a significant promotion. The idea of a lover commensurate with his own age and achievements began to interest him much more. It was not known what size his organ actually was, flaccid or erect, but his imagination of his potency had certainly changed. The change came about clinically through his bearing to free associate and realizing that the clinical dyad was functioning in a concerned listening way, so different from the fixed paranoia of big and little.

A young man, Mr E., presented in analysis with much anxiety which consisted of constantly asking questions. He demanded reassurance especially about his own self-diagnosis of an incipient psychosis. He constantly moved on the couch and preferred similarly constant mental movement, never settling into a topic which would alight on his mind. In a sense, his analysis was almost a total resistance to authentic free association. He had a history of his father walking out of the family when he was eight years old. But the story was told as if he had already made the adjustment needed for his understanding of this in his thought processes. It seemed that he saw the task of analysis as knowing more and more about the analyst and in particular trying to pin down my analytic attitudes, especially his expectation of my diagnosis of him. Not indulging him with answers and assurance was treated with caustic disdain, and he continued to start and end sessions with questions. Without knowing much of the meaning of all this, it certainly had the quality of an attack on analytic work and myself, as well as an intensity of antagonism from the beginning of analysis.

I did understand that the patient had hardly spoken in any depth about his life or history. The present tense of his difficulties seemed much more alluring and seemed to be the definition of his expectation of the work of analysis. On several occasions, I interpreted not just his disinterest in his historical life but how he was intent on keeping up a constant movement of evasion and on remaining with his questions in the present. In one session, he began with a dream fragment of suede shoes. He remembered that his mother had recently wanted him to have a suede jacket. Mother gave to him continuously and he took continuously from her. Again, his preference was to be in present time, and I interpreted this in an attempt to block the usual easy path of his resistance. To his surprise, he then said, "There was something very wrong with my legs when I was born". He remembered that he needed to be in a fixed harness, like some kind of callipers, for many months, so that the defect in his body could mend. He began to think about what he was saying. He realized that despite it being in the first year or two of his life, it was also an extremely potent metaphor of his intense hatred of any sense of restriction. Then he had struggled to move and it was impossible. Eventually, he would go very still and watch, only moving his eyes. He further associated that his mother had had a stillbirth prior to being pregnant with him. This had apparently led her to being in bed "for nine months of the pregnancy not moving". Here we see an intensification of atmosphere of severe and actual historical restriction. The patient had a thoughtful realization of the importance for his freedom of thinking and remembering.

The constant psychical and mental movements he had been displaying on the couch and in his life could now be begun to be understood as a near total psychosomatization of a fixed rigidity in his body enharnessed in leg callipers to prevent movement. Not only was it likely that his mother was rigid in fear for her unborn baby, but also her born baby was not able to move despite initially struggling. With immense frustration, he was able to watch, and this made clearer his addiction to films and his preference for watching and imagining a filmic life for himself away from reality. He was constantly on the move as a defence against being trapped and immobilized. This too was his powerful unconscious fear of analysis—that he would be fixed like an insect pinned to the couch unable to move again.

The suede shoes dream fragment was likely to have contained a representation of his traumatic early life. The opposite of soft shoes is the hardness of leg callipers fixing his legs rigidly. The patient brought his profound early trauma in his physical posture and constant movement on the couch. He also brought his fear of being trapped and re-fixed again—psychoanalysis would appear to be another set of callipers. In addition, he brought his fear of being trapped again by trying always to stay in the present tense of his life. Understanding his resistance to the analytic task of free association now became the royal road for the discovery of the psychosomatic disposition of his life.

The analytic task for Mr E. was to realize the depth of his early deprivation, his intense clinging to mother, his great anxiety about moving from his fixed body and mind, together with the emotional pain such realization released. The departure of his father when he was eight could now be seen as a much later event and one that could include a capacity to move perceivably to a more healthy mental space. His contempt for a leaving father, which he kept finding in the gaps between sessions, was in fact a cover for his need to repudiate the unconscious perception of the deeper significance of his mother pinning him down. In addition, he experienced an intense fear that if he moved away from the mother's control, he might damage himself too much and be fixed, alone and unable to move—a position he must have constantly endured by himself when mother was out of his gaze. His rage for father leaving covered his terror of being left with his restricting mother.

Near the end of his diary, Ferenczi wrote that as well as a need for "a capacity to integrate the fragments intellectually, there must also be kindness, as this alone makes integration permanent" (Ferenczi 1932, p. 207). This is undoubtedly a statement against the supremacy of an intellectual analysis alone. However, in some analytic communities, this form of treatment may be more common as analytic material is reshaped within the intelligence of a pertinent interpretation, as if the work is done by interpretation alone. Freud shrewdly recognized the need for working through. For Ferenczi, this would converge with the necessity to include consideration of the body. After all, the body of the infant requires caring for in a good enough scenario—a physical holding that is sensitive without making an adult sexual demand on the body. The analyst's awareness of boundaries means being able to include the body of the patient without the fear of it heralding movement towards assault and incest.

There is, of course, a negative side to the attitude of clinical kindness. Such clinical material points to the variability of being available at times to be closer or more distant in the transference–countertransference. This can vary from session to session and, of course, within a session. Sometimes the analyst will mistake the given intensity of the space until he has learned about the optimum mood for a given situation. Here, Ferenczi's concept of the elasticity of the transference is a valuable tool in regulating the parameter of closeness–distance via tact (Ferenczi 1928, p. 99). It is akin to the analysand arriving to enact the tale of the Three Bears. Either things are too big or too small and everything is awful until one can find the right fit. I am not arguing that the aim of analysis is to find some nirvana state of total understanding for the patient. Rather, that knowing more about the deep dynamics of what did not fit from the past, through trauma and *après coup*, enables the analysand to find a more comfortable state of relationships in the present and future.

In order to come closer to the early terrible experiences contained in the body, enough of a relaxation in the body is required. Georg Groddeck in his Baden Baden Spa tried to discover ways of enabling such bodily repose in his advocacy of baths and massage. Groddeck was a German physician who was one source for Freud's concept of the "Id" and has been referred to as the father of psychosomatic medicine. He established his own sanatorium, which was visited by both Freud and Ferenczi, and in 1923 Freud considered being treated and analysed by Groddeck (Fortune 2002, p. 33). Relaxation in the body in itself will not be sufficient, other than as a background atmosphere, as the act of trauma needs to be discovered in the transference–countertransference in order for it to be defused and elevated from its binding in the body to a safe passage into emotional language in the clinical dyad. Yet a patient in a relaxed body may be better able to deal with regression. In the first clinical case, Miss A., knowing me as a contraceptive in order to prevent the birth of some deeper emotionality, is an example of an act of murder in the transference, signifying, in all likelihood, the mother's previous attempt to abort her daughter and the subsequent symbolic murder by abandonment in her adolescence.

I make a plea to take the body of the patient as seriously as the mind and language. As Ferenczi eloquently remarked: "One needs to have lived through an affective experience, to have, so to speak, felt it in one's body, in order to gain conviction" (Ferenczi 1912, p. 194). I offer a brief clinical vignette about being in the body prior to ending the chapter. Several hospital departments had seen a patient as his buttock pain was unswerving in its intense chronicity. No medicine had any effect. Eventually, the specialist pain clinic referred him to the psychotherapy department for a psychodynamic interview. For the first time, the patient was asked what had been happening in his life at the onset of symptoms. The instant reply was that he had been attending his father's funeral. At once, a free-associative thought occurred to him: "My father was such a pain in the arse." The aftermath of such a revelation was that, although the pain was not instantly made to vanish, the patient, knowing its origin in his acrimonious relationship with his father, became much less concerned with something the matter in his body. In a way, he had no need to continue searching in hospitals for the completion of his mourning.

Aharon Appelfeld was pitched into a nightmare world without kindness. If the body is to be reclaimed from the clutches of deep defences, a relationship that recognizes and revives the traumatic position in order to develop a psychical growth from a bodily regression is essential in order to allow affect to have an unconsciously freer path into the mind. For Appelfeld, writing with a facility with words and their emotions became his creative pathway to survive.

CHAPTER SEVEN

Somatic resistance to termination: the contemporary use of "active" technique

In Europe no one knows how to scream anymore ... since they do nothing but talk.

—Artaud (1936, p. 75)

Miss A. never really wished to end her analysis. She had been in analysis five times a week for nine years. Much work had been achieved, and she had developed from being a gauche, hypochondriacal, and shy young woman to obtaining a prestigious senior management position and getting married. Analysis had reached a plateau. It worked, it was ongoing, but a deep sense of unconscious stuckness pervaded the atmosphere. Reviewing my countertransference over a period of time elucidated my boredom. So much work had been done. Her early obsessional symptoms had been worked through, leading to greater maturity and a more settled object choice. Unconscious guilt had been faced in relation to her parents and siblings, and her passive fatalistic acceptance of life had given way to a thoughtful, active marriage in which interpersonal difficulties could be spoken about, argued, and dealt with. Yet the ennui in the clinical spectrum pointed to the missing piece of the analysis; the necessity of a real ending.

125

This had, of course, been mentioned over the years, but her parent's departure for a life in a far-off country when she was just seventeen clearly bequeathed the spectre of fear of its repetition. Her feelings about loss, then and now, had been examined with care and concern at several points in the analysis. When her family left for a new life abroad, she had found the family of a school friend who were pleased to look after her during the period that she was sent to boarding school. Contact with the faraway family was very sparse. Miss A. never felt really loved or wanted by her mother. The younger siblings were always more privileged. She regarded her father as always taking his wife's position, no matter how odd. The fear of being left had been a central theme in her development, leading Miss A. to live in a private retreat, having few expectations about other people. This atmosphere of passive isolation had been well analysed to the extent that Miss A. had become able to speak up and know that everyone did not behave by leaving her as she had once imagined. Now a realization came into my mind that my constructions and words about the necessity for an ending had never really been accepted. Rather, it now appeared that she regarded "ending" as some sort of "analytic rule" that, at some time but not yet, an analysand would need to leave treatment. In the sessions, we began to recognize Miss A.'s delusional idea that if the analysis progressed and she was "doing well" that, in itself, would prevent a move towards the finale.

What had evoked my feelings of ennui? At this time in the analysis, the sessions seemed to empty out into long tracts of silence. Miss A.'s reluctance to think about ending analysis became the predominant theme over some weeks. It was tinged with her contempt for the idea of needing to work through an ending. As Freud has commented, "the ego treats recovery itself as a new danger" (Freud 1937, p. 238). As ending became the central focus of the work, it meant that interpretations about the ending could no longer be elided over, or accepted and then quietly rejected. Yet her idea that work would just suddenly stop was curious as she was well versed in analytic literature. She had a conceptual framework of a beginning, middle and end phase to an analysis as well as the idea of the return of the repressed.

It was very difficult to work out a final date. Despite acceptance by both of us that analysis had reached a state that felt like dull repetition, Miss A. was wary and resentful about this stage of our work together. The only piece of work that we both felt had not been explored was the actual end part of the analysis. It would be wrong to say that this state was fashioned by either of us, rather that together we began to know that the predominant atmosphere was about ending. Over a period of several weeks working together, we set a date one year ahead in the middle of a week and agreed by us both. Miss A. insisted that the date should not be an ordinary time moment, such as the end of the week, or a term. Even when setting this date had been achieved, we both had difficulty remembering it. For the next few weeks, the patient duly ignored the date, even though she had chosen it herself. Any interpretation I made in this area was emotionally received by Miss A. as a wooden textbook creation essentially unconnected to her, despite her choice of date and intellectual understanding. I felt that we must work through the ending or she would decide just to stop attending.

During the next period of analysis, Miss A. began to express a return to an intense anxiety about having diarrhoea or vomiting. Her journey to the session was fraught with immense concern that neither would be contained and that she would be embarrassed and humiliated by an eruption at one or other end of her gastro-intestinal system. Her body and her fear of its explosive disintegration became the uppermost strand of work, which seemed construed to disallow any words or thoughts about her rage over the impending ending. This type of material had figured in the analysis several years before, mainly related to her mother's hatred of disorder. At that time, Miss A.'s vomiting had been understood as representing a rejecting mother, something that I was now being perceived as, whilst the ending was in focus. It raised great doubts about the efficacy of all her analysis in Miss A.'s mind, as she began emotionally to deteriorate. My interpretations that her acute somatic relapse was a defence against her feelings about loss, of her analysis and of me, were intellectually accepted but emotionally vapid.

Miss A. was able to agree with me about her immense suppressed rage but was unable to feel it. Intellectually, she was prepared to understand her bowel anxiety in this way, but the somatic expression of her anxiety continued unabated. Her resistance was very high and lay behind her intense anxiety about arriving for and departing the session, which was always accompanied by Miss A.'s fear of psychosomatic breakdown. Her sessions were suffused with her fear of vomiting. She was very worried about the idea of suddenly having to get up from the couch in order to vomit, and there was a general feeling of wretchedness in the session. I realized that her growing fear of vomiting was leading to her not speaking, as keeping her mouth shut meant that she would be less likely to throw up. She wanted to spew her rage all over the long analysis and me. Miss A.'s symptom now stood in the way of free association with words. As her rage mounted, I invited her to consider moving from her fear of vomiting to re-locating her distress-rage by screaming in the consulting room. For several sessions, Miss A. speculated about my madness; she wondered if I was a discredited analyst and looked me up on the internet to see if she could find any clue about my being any good in my work.

At home in the evenings, she practised screaming in front of her encouraging husband. This ended up in her returning to my consulting room and shouting that I was "a wanker" (masturbator). It was as if by allowing herself to swear at me, she might be able to avoid having to scream.

What was the theory behind the particular direction I took in this treatment prior to the ending? Months had gone by and the patient's resistance and rage about ending was extremely high. Miss A. had been thinking about avoiding the ending by just stopping attending and leaving me, by projection with the experience of being walked out on. But she was also concerned that nine years of treatment would then give way to a serious failed analysis if she could not find a way of emotionally connecting with her affect, rather than somatizing to avoid the emotional pain of departure. Ferenczi's "active therapy" came to my mind. His idea was, and is, to enable a patient by means of certain artifices to comply more successfully with the rule of free association, thereby to assist or hasten the exploring of unconscious material. I think that Ferenczi's intuition was towards a clinical position that attempts to break through an intense resistance, a position that includes such concern for the patient that something has to be risked. This is very different from an analyst insisting that his task is to continue to interpret the patient's negativity. Whilst the resistance is not at all in doubt, this interpretative repetition may well be perceived by the analysand as indicating that the analyst is more and more out of touch with their state of mind. It is not unreasonable to think that it is around such profound moments that patients can and do drop out of treatment. Often, an analyst can blame this on the intense resistance of the patient. The idea that the stagnation of an analysis, with the patient prematurely ending, might be the fault of the analyst is harder to bear. Ferenczi's idea was to raise the clinical temperature in the analysis of the regressed patient as a way of becoming closer to the hidden affect beneath the resistance. If something can allow an eruption of the underlying feeling state, then with free association doing its work, analysis can move beyond the severe block imposed on it. Here active method is in the service of understanding the resistance more, being able to continue to develop analytic enquiry and, in the case of Miss A., move the analysis on so that she might mourn.

My invitation to Miss A. to scream was an attempt to get beneath an intense resistance, to deeply acknowledge and be able to work through ending. This was instead of staying passive and powerless as time ran out with the patient likewise being passive, with a wall of resentment between us. Miss A. remembered that when she was two years old, she screamed when out with her parents. She recollected that her mother just mocked her.

Ferenczi noted that activity worked "against the grain", that is to say, against the pleasure principle. These interventions are not comfortable. Freud had been forced into initiating an active framework to end the analysis of the Wolf Man (Freud 1918 [1914]). Ferenczi argued that active technique was not a return to banal suggestion or cathartic abreaction: "The provoking of an opposition by activity disturbs to no small degree the comfortable but torpid quiet of a stagnating analysis" (Ferenczi 1920, p. 212). The activity is not an end in itself. It is not so much about the cathartic discharge of affect, but the start of a deepening of the analysis beyond that moment. Ferenczi was concerned with authenticity in the clinical relationship, even when it meant understanding the requirement for dissent. This would be waiting to be understood in the unwrapping of early history.

Miss A. was very concerned that her treatment would leave her stuck and ill, and unconsciously wondered if I minded or cared. I felt that her state of resistance was also an attempt to ascertain whether I was fully committed to the project of her analysis. She now had considerable knowledge of the narcissistic complexity of her parents, who she viewed as never having had any real concern for her. In so many analyses, perhaps all, the last movement invariably returns to the beginning of the work. This is a concept readily understood in classical music, where the opening themes of the first movement of the symphony, despite being developed in subsequent movements, return to haunt again in the final movement. This is the totality of the particular musical journey as the major and minor themes struggle to find expression with each other throughout the various movements until the emergence of final resolution.

Miss A. had grown up feeling herself to be alienated from her mother, who became pregnant with her prior to marriage. Later, her desired younger brother had been more loved and cared for than she felt she had been. He had received expensive birthday presents, cars, the cost of his education, and expensive holidays, none of which had been offered to her. Her parents decided to send her away to boarding school despite being in the middle of her senior-level schoolwork. Later, she put herself through college, financially and emotionally unaided by her parents. Unsurprisingly, she did not feel loved by her parents.

Much earlier in her analysis, Miss A. had thought that her pregnant, unmarried mother might have attempted to abort her. She certainly knew she had been treated considerably worse than her younger, apparently wanted brother. Now, in the analytic ending, the word "termination" as a term for abortion took on its extra coloration in the transference. Similarly, her feeling of wanting to vomit could also be understood as an unconscious identification with an ambivalent pregnant mother.

There was an atmosphere of hide and seek in the work. Whilst Miss A. desired to hide her distress under her illness, I think she also hoped to be found and for her analysis to be completed successfully. Yet this is paradoxical because, for some patients, the very act of being found evokes an intense hatred precisely because the place of hiding, being alone there, has been discovered and compromised. She had the fear and the expectation that I would dump her as her parents had done previously during her adolescence. She had a deep-rooted phantasy that children only mattered if they fitted in with the adult. Parents could do what they wanted, and need not care about adolescents. To have a relationship with her parents then and now required giving up her own knowledge and mind and being in thrall to them both. This could just about be managed if she suppressed her rage. She had a transference expectation that I would treat her as her parents had and she must suppress her rage. That was and continued to be her historical reality. By remaining resistant to the meaning of the end of her analysis, she unconsciously believed she would avoid mourning and progressing into the depressive position.

Some five months before the ending, Miss A. brought a dream in which she was trying to change a baby's nappy. The baby was three months old, possibly had control over her bowels, and did not appear to need a nappy. A woman was helping her; she put the nappy on and then pants over the nappy. She said that she felt in a state of ambivalence, not wanting to know whether the baby had control over her bowels, even though she really did know that at three months babies did not have sphincter control. I interpreted that the work was about finding out that which was psychically real rather than staying in the arena of what must not be known and covered over. Miss A. responded with rage, wanting to kick down the doors in my consulting room and vomit all over my house. A little later in the session, she could say: "I know I am very angry at ending, but I feel that even though in the dream someone is by my side helping, it is ridiculous to scream." She continued by saying that she knew she had to do things herself and she did not trust me, or only trusted me a bit. If she were the analytic equivalent of being three months old, it would be absurd to be ending analysis, yet she knew that from the years of analytic work she was more psychically developed. I said, "In a few years time, you can say that you have had a good enough analysis but you never really trusted your analyst." She responded by saying, "Yes I know", and a fifteen-minute silence followed. She said, "I keep wanting to scream, but it is ridiculous and you will mock me". I responded, "You can say anything as long as you stay alone and by yourself." By this, I meant that she could be alone with her torturing thoughts and her fixed ideas.

The patient began a great scream with an intense long crescendo. Her body quivered. She grabbed the pillows alongside the couch and held them to her chest sobbing. She feared it was too much noise and quietened into a silence. She left the session looking very sad but saying that she was pleased to know that she was not stuck and alone. The scream had reached a climax that then passed over, leaving her feeling physically and emotionally relieved. After this, the patient returned for many sessions feeling lighter, pleased that we were working together rather than her being alone and now being able to speak much more freely about analysis, the ending, and her future. That she could notice that she did indeed have a future beyond analysis was a profound change, and to reach that point meant that she had had to relinquish her grievance about being left.

Some two months later, Miss A.'s repressed feelings returned with the emergence of a grievance. She stated that she was not ready to end, and she felt that I, her analyst, was not friendly. She complained that she felt unable to look at me at the start and end of sessions, as she felt too angry. Her capacity for free association led her to talk about a meeting between trainees and trainers, where many arguments were taking place. There had been a discussion about the difficulty of being in a senior position at work but without it really being discussed properly. They did not have her experience as she had been senior for several years now. She knew she had not been able to look at me at the end of the previous session, as she would have been too upset. She was still cross at the ending, but she knew if another year of analysis were offered, she would still have to face at some point her impossibility of ending. She said that she knew she turned away from important matters and could dig her heels in. She was cross I had opened the front door a few seconds late that day, but she did not want to get into an argument. I said, "Perhaps you were correct to have had a grievance for most of your life. You have spoken of how you experienced your mother and father as not caring about you, but why keep a grievance against the rest of the world? Your analysis, our work, will end and is it so strange that analysis ends?" Miss A. became very upset and cried copiously saying, "Yes, I know. It's the same situation with my best friend. She is busy so I see less of her. I can be angry or I can make more time for her." At the end of this session, she was able to look at me from the door and smile before leaving.

Clearly, she would have preferred continuing to be the junior to my senior position, continuing to be the subordinate analysand. In this session, perhaps we can see her pleasure in becoming a senior character in her own right, yet not feeling senior enough herself to let go of the analysis. What seemed to be missing from her unconscious was an idea that two people can both be "senior". Both being senior might be a recognition of the dynamics of grown-up children, who, whilst knowing they have parents older than themselves, have reached a time of also being grown up. Despite their age difference and genealogy, parent and offspring can have adult communications with both being grown-ups. Yet the register parent–child still continues alongside. There is a similar dynamic with an analysand who has nearly or completely ended their analysis. I think Miss A.'s unconscious work included working through the idea that if she was senior enough to finish, she needed to find a place in her mind for both of us in a new form. This had not been possible with her parents, as they had not shifted from the negative ways in which they had treated her throughout her life. Patients invariably have a hope that by being in analysis themselves, somehow parents will change towards them for the better. This may often be the result of analysis, due to the changing ways that the analysand is able to understand and alter their own dealings with parents, leading to some changes from parents in return. This may also not happen, leading to a deep sense of further injustice.

In the final few weeks of treatment, Miss A. and her husband went to visit her parents, who now lived distantly away. It was undertaken to examine what, if anything, might have changed over the years of her analytic work. After they had arrived, her father had insisted on downloading all her photos that she had taken on route, over a few days prior to seeing them. He was trying to be helpful to his daughter. With shock and rage, she discovered that he had managed to irrevocably wipe out all the photos. This was a clear example of her expectation and desire for her parents to change and her need to realize that her parents were much the same, despite her own psychoanalysis. Her father was unconsciously engaged in wiping out his daughter's life.

For Miss A., the early desire to be cared for in a better and different way from the one she perceived herself to have had led her to think, early in analysis, that the small window at the top of the house in which I had my consulting rooms was imaginatively hers. Thus as well as requiring space in my mind, she had a desire to be embodied inside my house. Perhaps this was an early sign of the embodied somatization that emerged/returned in the final movement of this analysis. Both her daydream and somatic symptoms were without affect and treated as just facts. It was sickening for her to imagine that not only would her analysis end, but also her safe haven would be disrupted. In the transference too, she would find herself homeless again. Clearly, a measure of her previous thinking capacity had been neutralized due to the emotional impact of a real ending. It needed to be discovered in the ending and had a profound meaning of fearing being abandoned again, like the imagined infantile abandonment that was repeated in her adolescence that left her to complete her last year and a half at boarding school, at a great distance from them.

Unconsciously, an analysand might be determining if the analyst is satisfied with the content and durability of the analysis or whether he reveals a sense of guilt that it is coming to an end. We need to discriminate between a decompensation at termination to irreconcilable complaint, or whether there is a real, tangible sense that enough solid ground work has been achieved.

Many analysts thinking about impasse material of the sort I have described will have their own ideas about which important interpretations should have been made, as if such interpretations could have broken the resistant block. It is perhaps hard to believe that other analysts, me in this case, have made a sufficient number and variety of interpretations in the direction of the present struggle and its relation to the past, the return of the repressed, attempts at control, and issues around sadomasochism, early trauma, ideas of exposing the failure of the analyst as dysfunctional parent, a split-off area to be maintained, and so on. Some analysts might understand an impasse of this sort as a clinical expression of the death instinct signalling that an analysis had reached bedrock. I view such an analytic position as a theoretical label over a complexity that with perseverance and tact can be further analysed. As Gilda De Simone perceptively writes: "I believe that there can be no doubt that an impasse and the phenomena connected with it are a disease of the relationship, for no other reason than the deep and sometimes total collusion induced by the analyst" (De Simone 1997, p. 44).

Marillia Aisenstein (2010, p. 465) writes of Lacan as "very critical of the classical technique of interpreting resistances. He sees it as a way of imposing on the patient a reality that is not his own, and which amounts to suggestion. The only value of interpretation lies in the associations it produces." He preferred the idea of interpretation as rocking the boat in order to disrupt meaning. For Aisenstein, interpretation "seeks a surprise effect which short-circuits secondary processes, aiming directly at primary process". Such would similarly apply to the disruption I caused my patient, in an attempt to find a place beneath the surface of her defences against the *après coup* of trauma.

The arena of this ending did throw into stark relief the difficulty of analysing the master/slave relationship whilst simultaneously being within it in the transference. In this analysis, the interpretation of the dynamics alone did not accomplish any psychic movement. Miss A. acknowledged that dynamic and understood its patterns intellectually but resisted the associated affective reverberations. Being able to scream enabled her to experience her affects rather than defending herself from her emotional pain, from the past in the present, about loss and ending.

Rickman, in his 1950 paper "On the Criteria for the Termination of an Analysis", pointed to a kind of "Irreversibility of a process of improvement in personality-integration and adaptability, which has been reached thus far ... that there will be no reverse process or regression on the cessation of treatment" (Rickman 1950, p. 127). He too comments on the wish of some patients to cling to the analyst and so perpetuate an infantile situation. By remaining as a child, the analysand can then ward off any sibling rivals who may be perceived as wanting to usurp their position on the couch. This was true for Miss A., as she had, despite much analytic working through, also constructed in her mind a safe physical haven, which she imagined would not survive the ending. It was as if her embodiment inside my house had to be maintained in a psychosomatic deterioration rather than her trusting the careful laying down of a new interiority inside her mind or relying on the efficacy of a new beginning. That new state would need to include her perception of her analysis and her analyst from outside the treatment room. The time beyond the termination, with her own internal sense of being senior too, would mean perceiving without illusion. This was the task that she had attempted to set herself to achieve with visiting her parents in the last few weeks of analysis and seeing them function beyond her illusion. A similar task awaited her in future life, beyond the analytic ending, to be able to examine life by herself, utilizing the working tools supplied during analysis. Working through the end with me went alongside having to face the painful reality that her parents, far away, were the same as ever, continuing to abandon her. It was important for her to understand that ending analysis did not have to have the same equivalence that I, too, was continuing to abandon her as well.

If I had allowed this analysis to comply with Miss A.'s silent unspoken rule that it must never end, my patient may have moved to a position of being highly critical and blaming me for my faulty technique. The blame transferentially must be laid at the analyst-parent's feet, even if the subject of ending is not raised. In the case of Miss A., my patient had embedded the trauma of feeling unwanted, as an abandonment that she absolutely expected would therefore happen again. This, I felt, could only be avoided through the sadomasochistic structure of the trauma being re-examined this time in the atmosphere of the final movement of the analysis. I wonder if there was also an unconscious preference for me to feel the affect, perhaps even be cross about the stuckness, as a form of enactment of identification with angry parents. In such a position, the patient would just be misunderstood, alone with her infantile fears about sickness and diarrhoea. Arguably, both sets of symptoms being about "getting rid of" can be viewed as evacuatory processes in which the idea of a scream would only be another variation. To my mind, this holds little validity precisely because the disruption led to psychic movement away from the fixity of her unconscious somatic position.

In testing the analyst during the termination, Ferenczi writes:

> It seems to me exceedingly probable that, when patients do these things, they are attempting to reproduce situations in which non-understanding educators or relatives reacted to the child's so called naughtiness with their own intense affectivity, thus forcing the child into a defiant attitude.
>
> (Ferenczi 1927, p. 83)

This paper was well regarded by Freud, who quoted it in *Analysis Terminable and Interminable* and agreed with Ferenczi's view that "among the factors which influence the prospects of analytic treatment and add to its difficulties in the same manner as the resistances must be reckoned not only the nature of the patient's ego but the individuality of the analyst" (Freud 1937, p. 247). In discussing the therapeutic difficulties in treating the Wolf Man, Freud writes: "... the pathogenic material consisted of pieces of the patient's childhood history and which now came away—the comparison is unavoidable—like sutures after an operation, or small fragments of necrotic bone" (ibid., p. 218). Freud had famously fixed a time limit on that analysis, which he described as a "blackmailing device" (ibid., p. 218), yet had to concede the failure of the ending with the continuation of the Wolf Man's analysis by Ruth Mack Brunswick. The metaphor of the emergence of fragments of necrotic bone as analytic associations is particularly interesting and poignant as this was exactly what Freud had contended with for many years living with cancer of the jaw. He had undergone many surgical procedures, undertaken by Dr Pichon, to remove necrosed bone, which by 1937, the date of his paper, was taking him closer to his death in September 1939.

Undoubtedly, Freud wrote pessimistically in regard to the therapeutic efficacy of psychoanalysis whilst at the same time knowing of his great difficulty in speaking due to cancer and the debilitating effect of his prosthesis, which Anna had to help him put in and remove daily. Treatment for his cancer was failing and clinical analysis was profoundly difficult for him to be able to manage. Freud was looking back at his clinical work spanning some forty-five years with profound uncertainty about what analysis managed to do.

Freud gave in his paper two clinical examples that had caused him "problems" in thinking about symptom resolution. The first of these examples is, without any doubt, a description of Ferenczi's analysis, with the complaint that it was unfinished. Freud writes:

> A certain man, who had himself practised analysis with great success, came to the conclusion that his relations both to men and women—to the men who were his competitors and to the women whom he loved—were nevertheless not free from neurotic impediments; and he therefore made himself the subject of an analysis by someone whom he regarded as superior to himself. This critical illumination of his own self had a completely successful result ... . But then, for no assignable external reason, trouble arose. The man who had been analysed became antagonistic to the analyst and reproached him for having failed to give him a complete analysis.
>
> (Freud 1937, p. 221)

Freud, the analyst in this treatment, defended himself by saying that at the time of the analysis, there was no sign of negative transference. Yet even if there had been some slight signs, in Freud's opinion, it "would have required some unfriendly piece of behaviour in reality on the analyst's part" (ibid., p. 222). Ferenczi had died in 1933, and four years on, Freud was still trying to resolve the conundrum of their technical differences during the last couple of years of their long collaboration.

One problem here seemed to be that Ferenczi could bear to take a particular analytic stance that might well be perceived initially as "unfriendly" in order to enable unconscious fragments to surface. Freud was more pessimistic about this position, as if it were an analytic interference. Freud had himself experimented with active technique by deciding to terminate the Wolf Man's analysis and thought of it as a therapeutic failure. Ferenczi was developing the idea of disturbing the patient to elicit more hidden material in order to interpret what may be of value for the regressed patient to think about and do. This line of thinking then moved into his concept of "elasticity". He writes: "Our 'active' mandate must therefore not be too rigid, but, as one of the colleagues whom I analyzed put it, be of an elastic compliancy" (Ferenczi 1925, p. 221). Ferenczi can be seen to have moved away from a rigidity and demand in the transference. "The analyst is first and last inactive and independent, and may occasionally encourage the patient to do particular actions. This clearly illustrates the difference between the 'active' analyst and the 'suggestionist'" (Ferenczi 1925, p. 224). The most important analytic activity was interpretation, in relation to the emergence of new material.

My patient certainly thought that in the last part of her analysis I was rather difficult and did not accept her idea that she could end analysis by leaving it without working through. Nonetheless, such unfriendliness, perhaps mirroring earlier parental affect towards Miss A., played a pivotal position in enabling a greater separation of unconscious parental imagos from the reality of separating from a real analyst.

Klauber noted that the longing for the analyst is not easily resolved. He commented that an aetiological factor in lengthy analyses is early maternal deprivation. However, he still believed that "Not many analyses are in fact interminable, as the patient always wishes eventually to stand on his own feet" (Klauber 1977, p. 63). Interestingly, Klauber writes that he would always hesitate before imposing any other termination other than one initiated by the patient. Termination by the analyst "can result in a trauma to the patient (and, I believe also to the analyst) which at the time the patient conceals. Only the patient's decision to terminate can assure for him the preservation of the precious identity he has acquired" (ibid., p. 73). Whilst I agree with much of this argument, I think it is important to recognize that there can be another position, so long as it is authentic. This occurs when the analyst-analysand work together in deciding the actual timing of the end of their work together. This is emphatically not one telling the other when the end must be, which can be redolent of parental control in the early and adolescent life of the analysand. Rather, it is a reconfirmation of the essential depth work between the analytic pair over many years. Working together acknowledges the future beyond analysis that can be authentically understood, not enacted, but accepted and developed. It is this sense of a shared experience that is remarkably absent in the traumatic early life of such patients. In a Winnicottian sense, the sort of ending I have described is a move from a demand–control system to a capacity to play which is not in the realms of sadomasochism. It is about two "senior" people working together with maturity.

Of course, it is relevant to examine, from the position of the analyst, whether there were countertransference issues in letting the successfully treated patient leave. Klauber regards some endings as being traumatic to the analyst. Clearly, I too was much affected by some of the material about ending. For a brief while, I also forgot and needed to re-find the date of the ending. A ten-year analysis with a patient one has become fond of and whose progress has been admired requires self-analysis to bear the ending as the patient goes to pursue his or her own life and desires beyond the couch. In addition, each termination of an analysis unconsciously re-evokes psychic positions in the analyst relating to his or her own endings and losses. Hopefully, such matters were part of the analyst's own analysis and their re-emergence will not be unexpected, nor should they impinge on the work with the patient.

It is important to examine why I utilized a scream as the potential transformational object to return the patient towards free association. Babies scream to indicate that something is the matter. This scream would not function in that way since it was already clear that something was the matter. Despite her mastery of work, adulthood, and marriage, Miss A. still desired to become pregnant. Her vomiting could contain a wish for pregnancy and her diarrhoea was then perhaps an equivalent for delivering a (shit) baby. Miss A. had stopped using contraception for some time as she and her husband wanted a baby, but she had not conceived. My inviting her to scream could be interpreted perhaps as containing the pleasure of the baby being born as, for example, herself being born beyond analysis at that same moment. The scream signified a real capacity to begin to end the analysis with a deep and authentic sadness meaning that she would then have to be born outside the analytic space she had been so determined not to give up.

Franco Borgogno, in a panel that included this paper (IPA Congress, Chicago, 2009), clarified Ferenczi's "analyst's activity", as searching for a way of making alive the frozen, dead, and agonic areas of the mind so as to let the patient (and sometimes even the analyst) reconnect to life and feelings. He underlined the example of the "role reversal" in the transference–countertransference dynamics as one of the most relevant points adumbrated in his work with deeply regressed patients. Borgogno added that the idea of the scream must have arisen from the analyst's preconscious perception that, for the patient to change and terminate the analysis, she needed to bodily integrate the dissociation of her infantile self, previously lived in her stead by the analyst (the role reversal). This suggestion to the patient functioned later as an "act of recognition", a sort of "Winnicottian gesture" (whose significance could often be found only in a second moment) more effective than mere words and interpretations and, finally, as an "act of freedom" for the analyst to be rescued from an entrapping interpsychic dynamics.

> Under this light, Sklar's solution should not be considered as an "acting out" since when the analyst is a "good enough analyst" there is much "working through" and "analytic work" underneath these actions, even if of course this "working through" and "analytic work" still needs to be further carried out in order to catch and understand the elements at stake in the analysis, and for the analyst to become for the patient someone who is really willing to take care and worry about him/her: in other words, to become a "new object", a new object for example, who "survives" in front of the patient's attacks not by adopting a nearly silent and still position but making his/herself heard.

> (Pontes 2010, p. 91)

Miss A. was able to stay for the whole of her long analysis. She did not leave prematurely. In her final session, she brought a large and beautiful orchid with a profusion of buds. It was a way of inviting the thought that she would be able to blossom beyond termination. Although she had not yet had a child, the orchids symbolized the beauty of such desire, and she talked about revisiting me at some time ahead when she would want to bring her baby to meet me. Her wish for my baby had been overcome by her knowledge of her now having her own husband and a very different family life of her own. So different from the small girl without hope for herself who had once, a long time ago, begun analysis. And how interesting, in the very last session, are these thoughts when put alongside her daydream from many years earlier: "*I met a two year old who had no parents, just at the top of the staircase. I thought of bringing her to you as she was crying. I wondered what you would think and I wondered how you would deal with it.*" Now she could imagine her own baby, not as herself in tears, alone without parents, but an analysed character who knew she had an analyst.

I am arguing about an important ambiguity at the heart of analysis where a choice needs to be made about considering resistance as being the final bedrock, or discovering a more nuanced state in which some way of moving beyond the impediment to further analytic understanding might be achieved. Both positions require the capacity to mourn. Once one has reached some sort of bedrock, whatever that is, mourning for not being able to change the world or oneself further is essential. To my mind, the understanding of this bedrock must include the capacity of the analysand to accept the necessity of mourning. It must not be experienced by analyst or patient as an achieved or final state. If there is a feeling that the analyst has not done enough or is felt to have failed the patient that is an indication for more work to be done, including in the transference. Bedrock, if it exists, should be a place accepted and occupied together. This means recognizing the bleak dead isolated landscape that is the aftermath of profound, near endless traumatic states leading the baby, child, and adolescent to develop by holding themselves alone without expectation of a caring, mindful object in the vicinity. I believe work must occur in such places to help the analysand eventually to recognize that in the ending of analysis, their analyst is not enacting a piece of the analysand's unacceptable and very painful past in all of its reality and phantasy, but that we have been available in the transference, in order to see, feel, and mourn in a new emotional construction. Perhaps recourse to psychosomatic defences in such cases of early neglect is a more common configuration at the end phase of analysis than is usually realized. This is why it is so important for the analyst to make every effort to find a way to the affect hidden beneath profound defensive somatization, a process that proved to be essential in order to end this particular analysis.

CHAPTER EIGHT

The life cycle of the psychoanalyst: reflections on a seminar for newly qualified analysts[1]

Jonathan Sklar and Michael Parsons

> *The use of the word "freedom" is one of the surest indices of the user's general ultimate ideal of life, of what to want and what to avoid … one of the most faithful indicators of where a man stands.*
>
> —Isaiah Berlin (2006, p. 207)

This chapter highlights the concept of the psychoanalyst's life cycle, extending from qualification, through the prime of an analyst's career, to retirement and beyond. The details of the life cycle emerged from the experience of leading a seminar to help recently qualified analysts think about the development of their analytic identities. Issues which first appear in the post-qualification period continue to present themselves in different ways throughout an analyst's working life. The idea of this life cycle has not been much articulated, particularly with regard to its later stages. Bringing an analytic career to a close raises practical and emotional questions which are not easy to discuss openly. Two ideas which are emphasized are, first, that the analytic life cycle needs to be seen as an organic whole and, second, that the external practicalities of an analyst's professional life need always to be considered in terms of how they express the analyst's internal sense of his or her analytic identity.

The idea that a psychoanalyst's career has its own particular life cycle has only occasionally been noticed in the literature, either explicitly (Dewald & Schwartz 1993; Gold 1988) or implicitly (Cooper 1986; Wallerstein 1981), and even these sparse references comment on the way that open discussion of the idea is avoided. One purpose of this chapter is to draw attention to the life cycle of the psychoanalyst as a concept. The working lives of analysts may take many forms, but within the variety there is a pattern, which evolves over the years with particular processes of development running through it. This life cycle extends from an analyst's qualification, through the milestones of a professional career, with its clinical work and its possibilities for involvement in training and other areas both within and outside the analytic institution, to its close, when the ageing analyst relinquishes those responsibilities and finally gives up the couch in the consulting room.

In the extensive literature on psychoanalytic training, qualification tends to be regarded as an end-point, not a beginning. Shane, however, has written of the progression from patient-candidate to analyst, from one who is nurtured and taught to one who nurtures and teaches and then goes on to consolidate their identity as analyst. It might be useful to conceptualize this latter as "analyst-hood as a developmental phase" (Shane 1977, p. 106). Szalita also comments pertinently: "Formally, one becomes a psychoanalyst when the graduation committee decides that the candidate is ready to start conducting analyses on his own. But in reality one is becoming an analyst for as long as one practices this exacting profession" (Szalita 1985, p. 134). Despite such statements, not much has been written about further developmental processes once the analyst is no longer in embryo and the life cycle proper is under way. Rosenbloom (1992) discussed the elaboration of the analyst's identity in the period after qualifying, and Fogel & Glick (1991) described a post-qualification group, which systematically re-read Freud as a catalyst to the development of its members' identities as analytic teachers. Both articles rightly stress the importance of the first years after graduation. Our emphasis here, however, is on the cathexis of an analytic identity as a lifelong issue for psychoanalysts.

Occasional articles touch on identity issues in the later stages of an analyst's career (Cooper 1986; Ellman 1996) but with regard to the ageing analyst and the closing of an analytic life, a paper such as Michaels and Schoenberg's (1966), about when training analysts should retire, is noticeable amid the overall silence. It is not that analysts are not concerned with such topics. Conversation at analytic gatherings shows how much analysts do think about them as they get older and psychoanalytic institutions may face difficult situations with elderly analysts who are unwilling to recognize that they need to give up work. But to discuss openly and write about old age, retirement, and the possibility of physical and mental deterioration, so as to think about what they mean for a psychoanalyst's analytic identity, does not seem an easy matter. Rather, it can be regarded as an unwelcome topic, something that can be mentioned but not taken seriously enough to develop best practice within an analytic society. Resistance runs high.

For several years, Michael Parsons and I ran a group for newly qualified analysts in the British Psycho-Analytical Society. Our experience of this group has prompted us to reflect on how an analyst's awareness of what it means to be a psychoanalyst develops over the whole of the analytic life cycle. If ageing and the end of one's working life are thought of in isolation, without being related to the rest of that cycle, they have no meaning in a larger context and may well inspire dread and avoidance. The importance of seeing the analytic life cycle as a whole is therefore one conclusion that we wish to present. A second important theme is that, while the practical aspects of organizing an analytic career take different forms as the career evolves, those essential practicalities go on needing to be understood, from the beginning to the end of the cycle, in terms of how they express externally one's internal sense of identity as a psychoanalyst.

A seminar for newly qualified analysts

Training in any psychoanalytic institute is a complicated business, exciting and sometimes frustrating. However infuriating, infantilizing, or even persecutory one's particular experience might feel at times, there is support from personal analysis, from supervisors and seminar leaders and from belonging to a student group. Above all, as a student you know what you are there for. Then suddenly, the goal is realized and the years-long quest for one's psychic desire is over. There is pleasure in the success and relief at the achievement. But overnight, all that structure that has been so supportive, confirming, and sustaining disappears. One is now something called "a psychoanalyst" but just at this point when it is most necessary, there may be little help in finding out what that means or how to set about being it, beyond one's analysis, which may or not be still ongoing.

In view of this, we set up a seminar group in the British Society to try and help recently qualified analysts think about how their identities as psychoanalysts might develop. The first group met for three years in the early 1990s and the second group met regularly from 1996 until it ended in 2004. All new analysts were invited to join the seminar when they qualified. Some declined, glad of their new freedom from institutional matters and wanting to give fuller attention at last to family and other commitments. Others welcomed a space to think about the next phase of their professional life. There was a rule that nobody stayed for longer than three years; fostering dependence was the last thing we had in mind. The group's members varied, of course, in how they handled the leaving of it, but the move almost always marked a distinct step forward in their assumption of an autonomous analytic identity and increasing clarity about the future direction of their analytic work.

The seminar met once a month for ninety minutes. Its theoretical stance was based on Balint's (1957) groups for general medical practitioners and the method of work is by free association around the idea of what it means to be a psychoanalyst. There was no set topic for discussion, and participants brought thoughts and feelings arising out of any aspect of their professional lives. Clinical situations were sometimes mentioned, if they posed questions for the analyst about his or her analytic functioning, but the aim of the seminar was emphatically not to be a clinical or supervisory workshop. Unconscious group processes inevitably showed themselves. Alongside Balint's work, Bion (1961) is another reference point, although the group is not conducted like the therapeutic groups he described. At times, the work might appear superficially to be group-analytic in nature. Long silences were not uncommon and there were attempts to treat the leaders as authority figures or to draw us into teaching or supervisory positions. We expressed clearly, however, that the seminar consisted of a group of colleagues, not of analysts and analysands or supervisees. Interpretations were not made in terms of group process, for this might lead the seminar away from its primary task of helping members reflect on their identities as psychoanalysts. This is what our intervention as leaders of the group always aimed to promote, by facilitating the group's free association.

An important task during the period after qualification is the shift from regarding the training institute and teachers as those who know what being an analyst means, to locating that knowledge within one-self. The British Society is one of those bodies that require candidates to be in analysis until qualification and many continue their analyses for some time afterwards. In analytic institutes that do not have the same requirement, personal analysis may have ended before qualification and so not be available to help in working through this shift. Almost always, the seminar's members are still in analysis when they join it, but the question of when to end their analyses was present and many of them did so while in the seminar. Members varied in how much they talked about this, but it meant, firstly, that themes of fulfilment and disappointment, loss and ending, which pervade the working life of an analyst, were inevitably present and, secondly, that the progressive internal self-authorization of its members' analytic identities became an important concern of the group.

This gives an indication of how, although the seminar focused on a particular phase in the development of an analyst's identity, themes kept cropping up in it, which permeated the life of an analyst, from qualifying, through the prime of one's career, to retirement and beyond. The work of this seminar, to do with the problems and preoccupations of the period immediately after qualification, was our starting point. Our wider interest, however, and the overall subject of this paper, is the lifelong evolution of those issues, from the beginning of an analyst's working life through to its end.

Three significant stages in an analyst's career are the period after qualifying, the middle phase, and the approach to, and aftermath of, retirement. We focus on these in turn, but there are no clear divisions. Analysts' lives evolve gradually, continuously, and in all sorts of differ-ent ways. We also mention certain milestones, such as becoming a full member of one's society and becoming or not becoming a training ana-lyst, in relation to issues that these steps may bring into the foreground. Our own experience is drawn from the British Society, but there are significant differences to be aware of between analytic institutions. The status of training analyst may have very different meanings from one society to another, and not all societies have the distinction between associate and full members. Many analysts, of course, develop their careers in ways that do not involve these steps in any case. Nonethe-less, we believe the issues we address are ones that analysts in every country, and whatever the particular local context of their work, are in some way faced with.

Early years

The recently qualified psychoanalyst is concerned with all sorts of practicalities about how to establish and run an analytic practice. But over and over again, we observed that what present themselves as practical issues in the external world can only be managed by understanding how they relate to an analyst's internal sense of his or her analytic identity. The many different settings in which it is possible to embark on analytic work challenge preconceptions about what being an analyst means. There is the "analytic setting" itself, of sitting with an individual patient four or five times a week for as many years as it takes. Many newly qualified analysts want this to be the basis of their working lives; most want to do at least a certain amount of it. But many also have a strong commitment to their country's public health service and want to find ways of being analysts in that context. This can be difficult, because there is no classically accepted view of how to be an analyst away from the couch. Analysts working in health service contexts do an important job in representing psychoanalysis publicly and bringing the benefit of analytic understanding to the community. Developing one's identity as an analyst outside the consulting room demands particularly strong internal confidence. Either situation calls for a constant bridging between the external representation and the internal awareness of what it is to be an analyst.

A factor with its own particular significance for an analyst's life cycle is the gender of the analyst. This has both psychobiological and psychosocial aspects. Women psychoanalysts face the same issues as other professional women regarding the demands of work and family life, and these may influence the kind of work situation a woman analyst chooses. Gender can enter into questions of institutional power and influence—less so probably in psychoanalysis than in some other professions, but there may still be an effect on how men and women analysts perceive the career options available to them. There is a considerable literature on pregnancy in the analyst, tending to discuss it more for how it affects the patient than for its role in the analyst's life. Some articles do come near the question of what it means for a woman to be a mother and a psychoanalyst at the same time (Dewald & Schwartz

1993; Etchegoyen 1993; Imber 1990). But it may be hard for these two aspects of a woman's sense of her identity to find their true relation to each other, through the maze of external practicalities (work space in the home, job-sharing in institutions, child care arrangements) that are needed for their realization. Imminent fatherhood in a male analyst can undoubtedly have an effect on the analysis, but it does not show in the way that imminent motherhood does in a female analyst. Perhaps, because of this, the meaning for a male analyst of becoming a father and how this relates to his sense of identity as a psychoanalyst are topics hardly discussed in the literature at all. The question on the other side of the coin, of what it means for one's analytic identity if one does not have children, is also seldom mentioned. Being without children may be a matter of choice, or of private pain and sorrow. Individual circumstances are unique, but there must still be a difference between the psychic situations of a male analyst who is not a father and a female analyst who is not a mother. All these issues which relate to gender are sensitive ones. When they arose in the seminar (led as it was by two male training analysts), they were touched on gingerly, but with relief that it was possible to talk about such issues.

An immediate question, as one sets out on private analytic practice, is "How am I going to get patients?" The climate today seems more difficult and referrals harder to come by than in the past. But to embark on psychoanalysis has always meant a daunting commitment of time, energy, and money, and the perceived "crisis in psychoanalysis" may have a great deal to do with this question of external and internal identity. In a culture which is turned towards superficial, pragmatic, short-term solutions, where judging cost against externally measurable benefit is an almost automatic mind-set, how do we find people to embark on something that is based on an opposite attitude? Analysts may fall into a kind of despair about this which, when examined, turns out to be despair at convincing people that analysis will bring benefit in those pragmatic, external, show-me-what-I'll-get-for-my-money terms. One might well question how one can expect to get analytic patients on such a basis. A frequent topic in the seminar was the shift towards knowing from deep inside ourselves that we have something to offer, which operated at a quite different level from that. The point about working five times a week, for example, is not to demonstrate empirically that it produces different results from three times a week. Five times a week represents a unique kind of space available for a patient in the analyst's mind. We regularly observed that when the seminar helped new analysts recognize how the training has begun to make possible the internalization of this available space, analytic patients emerged after all. The prospective patient who comes for consultation to someone operating on this wavelength may sense that he or she is in contact with a particular kind of awareness and be willing to follow that, even without knowing, at that stage, quite what it is. A crucial element in finding an analytic patient is the conscious thought that that is what one wishes and is able to have. A colleague in the seminar said, "I have realized that one reason I haven't any analytic patients is that I have never asked anyone to refer them to me." Another said, "I had an insight—I have never really thought of myself as being able to have an analytic practice. As soon as I realized that, I could begin to see how there might be space in my mind for an analytic patient." There is hard external work in letting senior colleagues know, and going on reminding them, that one has a vacancy for analytic patients, and hard work also in developing that as an internal truth about oneself. Feelings of guilt about not having analytic patients may exist alongside an anxiety that claiming to be an analyst is a grandiose piece of presumption. Bringing these feelings into full consciousness is necessary, but often difficult, for the newly qualified ex-student.

The comment about consultations with prospective patients touches on the same point. New analysts may be doubtful about their ability to assess potential analytic patients, and the feeling can persist for some time of wanting patients to be referred with the seal of approval of someone more senior. This may be particularly so for non-medical analysts without an extensive background of clinical experience. Likewise, how do you know when it's all right to stop supervision? As a colleague ruefully reported in the seminar, one supervisor had said, "Of course you need to continue supervision", whilst at the same time the other was saying, "Stop supervision now; go and do your own exploring". Some analysts do need to continue supervision. Avoiding independence can also, however, become a way of life. Many paths are available: carry on as though nothing has happened; stop supervision and see what standing on your own two feet is like; have intermittent consultation with a senior colleague; seek out (or set up) a supervision peer group. All these have their attractions and their complications. One can, of course, simply decide whose advice to believe, but only an inward sense of where one has got to in the process of becoming an analyst can really help resolve these questions.

The material reality of the new analyst's consulting room has a powerful symbolic meaning. The most evocative analytic space one has known so far is the analyst's room on whose couch one has lain for hundreds of hours. That was shaped by another analytic mind. Now it is time to shape a space of one's own. In Britain, not many analysts are well established in private practice at the time they qualify, and the setting up of one's own room is often a particular landmark. Even for those who have already had rooms of their own, the significance of this space, now that they are psychoanalysts, has to be freshly discovered. There may be tangible, external practicalities and anxieties about finance and property dealings, or about rearranging the home. Minute details can matter tremendously. Do you need an entry phone? What sort of couch cover to have, where to stand when patients come in, and who opens the door when they leave? A particular kind of anxious joyfulness often surrounds these issues in the seminar, because the external event represents a major development in the internal realization of an analytic identity. Even if the consulting room is already a familiar space, there is a deepening realization of how it stands for an internal space which is now becoming available for analytic work. Understanding in this way what the consulting room means helps the new analyst in discovering how to make use of it. One important aspect of this is the solitude. The separateness of the consulting room marks an independence from the institution where one was a student, but it also brings aloneness. Buechler (1998) has written of the loneliness that particular kinds of patients may induce in the analyst, while Quinodoz (1996) and Cooper (1986, p. 592) emphasize that all analytic work demands a capacity for solitude. The new analyst has to bear the isolation which the busy training helped to avoid, and begin to discover what can grow in it.

Analytic fees constitute a difficult arena at any stage (Eissler 1974; Layland 1987), but particularly so for recently qualified analysts. They may have families to support and other commitments including, perhaps, debt from the years of training. Knowing how far there is still to go in becoming an analyst, they may doubt if they are entitled to charge realistic fees. Giving oneself permission to charge more than the fee paid to one's own training analyst is a milestone, especially if that analysis still continues. And what about the helpful senior analyst who refers a patient who can only pay a very low fee? Of course, the new analyst is grateful, but a referral that would pay a bit more of the mortgage would not come amiss! One may hear of eminent analysts who disapprove of a level of fee that, for oneself, is simply necessary in order to make ends meet. Do some people, who may have bought their houses long ago and have grown-up children earning their own livings, simply not know what life is like today? But it might feel dangerous to have such thoughts about those one depends on professionally. Complex institutional transferences may be involved. One's own anxieties, either about being arrogant and greedy or about undervaluing oneself, interact with fears about how one may be perceived by colleagues. This issue exemplifies the task of giving up both idealization and paranoia towards the analytic institution, and instead cathecting it by cathecting oneself as an analyst who is finding an identity within it.

The whole question of institutional relationships is a tricky one for the newly qualified analyst. Students have a clearly defined position and then, overnight, teachers become colleagues. Qualifying means joining a family with complex and ambiguous dynamics. The former student has to identify those family dynamics and find how to belong to, and contribute to, the society's life in a way that fits with the institution and is also meaningful for his or her own self. How anxious need one be about what one's peer group and senior colleagues think? How much can one afford to follow one's own ideas? Discussion in the seminar regularly brought up fantasies about other new analysts being better supported, getting more referrals, being invited to join committees, and so on. Gradually, all in the group come to realize that everyone has similar difficulties, anxieties, and fantasies to deal with. It was a relief, in the end, to recognize that being an analyst is a rewarding but difficult life for all of us.

It can be a surprisingly painful shock, though, as time passes since qualification, to discover that analysis does not stop being difficult. If the training is thought of as learning "how to do" analysis, students may have an expectation that once they have learned that, they will know it. However much we are aware, rationally, that qualifying is only the beginning, preconsciously that hope can be a strong one. As analysts become less newly qualified, they find that staying with the unconscious, their own and the patient's, goes on being very difficult and often painful. Psychic work is needed to accept that this is not something to be overcome; it is what the life one is embarking on consists of.

There is another theme that regularly appeared in the seminar, which extends forward, right to the end of one's life as an analyst. We have been struck by how often discussion in the seminar revolves around death. This is an area where unconscious meaning and external reality interact constantly. It is sad when colleagues die, immensely so when the death is tragically premature. It is especially traumatic for a student's training analysis to be cut short in this way. But death is an element in all analytic work and a student is faced with it by the very fact of emerging from the training. This sort of material often expresses the group's recognition of the death of the student identity. Ambivalence about letting go of that, to allow the birth of a new identity as a psychoanalyst, may involve a murderous attack, in unconscious fantasy, on the training analyst who has made this possible. In such instances, death may represent the idea of castration of the analytic mind. The world of fact impinges here again, however. With qualification nowadays often at the age of forty or fifty, half of life has in reality already gone. The dissonance of this can provoke black humour or depression. But it has to be worked through somehow. For all analysts, the relationship they develop to the knowledge of their own deaths is an essential element in their psychoanalytic identities.

Middle age

It is clear enough how these issues resonate throughout the working life of an analyst. But the experience of the seminar revealed still further how the issues, which are discussed in terms of the post-qualification period, do not get solved once and for all and disappear. They go on presenting themselves in new forms, and sometimes more acutely.

Newly qualified analysts have to work out, as we said earlier, a context for their analytic work. How much private practice, research, public health service, or university work to do? These all have their satisfactions, and their anxieties and frustrations. Whatever the sociopolitical situation in one's own country—and this, of course, varies widely—it will take time to find the right balance. Fortunately, there is time, early in a career, to do this. Then comes a moment when we look back and see that decisions have been made, some time ago now, and we realize that our path is set. It is one thing for young analysts to worry about getting patients. What about the older analyst, for whom it is now too late to do anything but private practice? New analysts may have fantasies about the fascinating wealthy patients that fill their senior colleagues' diaries, but the fear of not getting patients might be worse in mid-career than at the beginning. As time passes, and we have to live with being the kind of analyst we thought we wanted to be, such external practicalities need more and more to be sustained by the continuing development of internal trust in that analytic identity.

How to keep alive the freshness of what being an analyst means? For the recently qualified analyst, even if he or she does not yet know much about being an analyst, it is by definition something to discover. After fifteen or twenty years of analytic work, we know more about it. The problem then becomes how to maintain what Rilke called "your humble resolve to be always beginning" (1964, p. 21). When Oedipal structures have become so familiar and projective identification so recognizable, we may be challenged still to re-find an emotional reality in our quotidian interpretations. Experiencing the power and, especially, the affect, of an interpretation, is not just something for the patient. It is by knowing those in himself or herself that an analyst is able to keep rediscovering the reality of the unconscious. If our formulations, from being familiar, become routine, not only will the patient find it hard to come alive, but we shall be less alive as well, emptier, drier, eventually perhaps even coming to resent what being an analyst has turned into. Cooper's description of the "burnout syndrome" (1986) in psychoanalysts is telling.

So it is important, in the middle phase of one's career, to go on seeking nourishment for one's analytic identity. New sources of it do indeed open up at this time. But the internal work that was done earlier, in the years following qualification, now turns out to be crucial for how one can use those sources. If a psychoanalytic society distinguishes between associate and full membership, progression from the former to the latter is a significant developmental step. Increasing experience opens more doors to involvement and responsibility in the life of the Society. But full membership, for example, may be sought, or not, for all sorts of different reasons. If one's confidence as an analyst is not developing very well, putting oneself forward for it may attract welcome support but at the same time increase one's anxiety about failure. Will certain important people think it odd if one does not aspire to it? If the idea does not feel genuine, can one feel secure enough not to have to? To stay aware of one's real needs and look for help with them if necessary, to trust the analyst one is becoming, even if it is not what others expect—these are difficult tasks.

Committee work, teaching, research, and other kinds of involvement in the life of one's society are potentially very generative. But if they are to be truly nourishing to one's analytic identity, the internal meaning of such work is again important. This will depend on what kind of internal relationship to the analytic family it has been possible to make. If we appreciate our societies as organizations that help us to identify and value ourselves as analysts and show us how to help others do the same, then helping them to become more and more that sort of organization will deepen and enlarge our own sense of ourselves as analysts. But what if the relationship to one's society still has a lot of idealization, or persecutory feeling, mixed up in it? Then a sense of freedom in deciding how involved to be in the society's life would not come easily. Instead of choosing, an analyst may be driven, either to distance himself from it, or to take on commitments out of narcissistic wishes or the need to placate a guilt-inducing superego. If those internal projects fail and the safety or gratification that was hoped for is not found, then instead of being nourished, there is a sense of being let down by analytic life. This is crucial in the area of training. The development from being a student, nurtured by the training, to becoming a part of that provision, supervising and giving lectures and clinical seminars, is an important advance in a professional career. But it needs to be more than that, for the teacher as well as the students. Teaching can help the teacher to stay analytically alive, provided it is itself an expression of that development. When this is the case, teaching can become the transmission, in whatever theoretical or clinical form, of what it means to evolve an analytic self.

There may be other members, however, of one's analytic family who have arrived at very different understandings of psychoanalysis. Allowing and appreciating difference seems to become progressively more important as a working life goes on. This is not just a matter of theoretical viewpoints. Questions of clinical technique may open up much sharper divisions than purely theoretical issues. It calls for maturity to bear these differences and to transmit one's own understanding without necessarily wanting students to arrive at the same view. A colleague spoke with concern, in the post-qualification seminar, about how hard it can be not to become a clone of other analysts' ways of working. It is a continual and vitally important challenge to our development as analysts that the fact of difference and the being of oneself as an analytic character should bring enrichment and not an impoverishing doctrinal separateness.

As analytic life progresses, the judgement of one's peers comes increasingly to the fore. In institutes where it is a mark of elite status to be accredited as a training analyst, applying to become one is, in that respect, a most formidable decision. Students are evaluated by those far above them in an institutional hierarchy. For all the infantilization they may complain of, there is something reassuring about having the lines so clearly drawn. Where full membership is to be assessed, the judges are still senior, but there is more at stake. The associate member is now exposing his or her work as a qualified professional. Assessment to become a training analyst may regressively reactivate a transferential sense of judgement from on high, but in reality the discussion at this stage is between potential equals. Presenting a case at this level means saying to one's evaluators, "This is where I have got to, and I think it puts me on a par with you". To commit oneself to that statement is daunting and analysing as best one can the anxieties it arouses is all part of preparing to be a training analyst. We shall see in due course how the need to bear the judgement of peers comes round again at the end of a working life.

The turn of the wheel, from having a training analyst as a student, to being one with student analysands of one's own, brings into sharp focus the question, which faces all psychoanalysts, of what happens to their identifications with their own analysts. How like our own training analysts, or how different from them, shall we be with our students? The candour needed for open discussion of such questions is not easy, but Smith (2001) has shown how, throughout an analyst's career, identifications with analysts, supervisors, and other mentors can either hamper or nourish one's clinical practice. This connects also to other questions. How like our parents, or how different from them, shall we be with our own children, if we have them? The path of an analyst's working life continually reflects the issues that brought him or her into analysis in the first place.

Death looms larger at this stage. When our own analysts die, usually in the middle of our careers, they no longer stand between us and our own deaths. The mind in which we know we lived so intensely no longer exists. Supervisors and other important teachers and mentors may die. We may have to bear the death of close friends. Thoughts of our own death, and questions about what our contribution will really have amounted to, become more insistent. Colleagues age, becoming frail and less able to work, and we wonder how we shall cope with the end of our own lives as analysts. We realize that one day we shall not be able to take our functioning as analysts for granted any longer. At this point, there is particular need for a strong and secure internal sense of our analytic identities. Otherwise, commitments may be taken on, valuable and productive perhaps for one's institution or in career terms, but which don't quite bring the satisfaction that was hoped for, because fundamentally they are antidepressants rather than expressions of our analytic selves.

Twilight

The seminar we have described was for analysts at the beginning of their careers. In it, they shared the excitement, anxiety, and anticipation that qualifying brings. It would be valuable and reassuring to know that there was somewhere to discuss the close of life as an analyst with others in the same situation. One hopes that, at that time, there will be a sense of satisfaction and fulfilment, the rewards of a life spent doing fascinating and useful work. But there are also anxieties, and sometimes difficult decisions, at a time of life when, for many reasons, one may be feeling increasingly alone. The analysts, however, who might know that experience from having lived and worked it through to the other side of it, are not there. This brings sharply home how hard it may be to face truly the closing of one's analytic life. Very little has been written about this, as we commented earlier, but the resonances and interrelations already noted between different phases in an analyst's career suggest some thoughts about how the beginning and the ending of it may relate to each other.

"The end of one's life as an analyst" is an ambiguous phrase. Does it refer to professional retirement; the end of one's working life? Or does it mean, simply, the end of one's life: that one is a psychoanalyst facing death? The nature of psychoanalysis makes it impossible to be an analyst without an involvement of one's whole self in the work. When analysts retire, and the practice of analysis that has absorbed so much of them is no longer available, there are questions to face. What personal identity remains to sustain one in one's last years, so that one can think, with acceptance, "Well, being an analyst was good, but now I'm not one any longer"? Or can there be meaning in the idea of still being a psychoanalyst—not having been, but still being one—even when one cannot do what an analyst does any more?

If these questions have only negative answers, the prospect of life after retirement may be deathlike, and the terror of this may make it hard for some analysts to give up their work when in reality they need to. Alongside its primary function of helping the patient, the work of analysis meets needs in the analyst. This is well recognized. But for an ageing analyst, the need to go on having patients can become an area of vulnerability. There may be fear that, as the consulting room closes, the internal space of analytic understanding, which it represents, will also close. If listening analytically to patients is when analysts feel they are most profoundly and creatively in touch with their own selves, and if they do not know how else to find those levels in themselves, then giving up that work will be a desolate prospect.

If there are positive answers to those questions, however, the possibility opens up of a mirroring between the beginning and the ending of a career. The group for newly qualified analysts is ostensibly about beginnings and time stretching ahead. But we were surprised, as we have already said, to find how much the group talked about death. All analytic work involves, at some level, confronting the fact of death, and one cannot be fully alive without knowing its inevitability. The opening of one's analytic career already contains, somewhere, an awareness of its close. When that close comes, time stretches mostly behind and the psychic work is ostensibly about endings. The developmental challenge at this stage is to discover what kind of beginning that ending can contain and how to recover for oneself the time that has been given to others. This must depend on relinquishment. For the student finishing training, and particularly when the training analysis comes to an end, there is a necessary process of disillusionment. Yes, the training was very good, but there is such a lot one did not get from it. Recognizing the failures in our personal analyses can be very painful. But the future beckons; there is time to fill in the gaps and make good the lacks. For the analyst at the close of his or her career, however, the reckoning is final. That was the life one chose. Its disappointments and frustrations cannot be remedied and the contributions one did not manage to make will never now be made. Even if fulfilment and satisfaction are there in full measure, it is still poignant when the work that produced them has to be laid aside.

How much does one still strive, towards the end of a working life, to keep renewing the sense of oneself as an analyst? One will have, after all, a tried and serviceable way of thinking and working. It might seem attractive just to go on doing what we know we can do for as long as we can do it. The risk, though, if one approaches the ending with a sense only of the sands running out, is of a gradual internal depletion. If, on the other hand, we do try to keep refreshing our analytic identities up to the end, the pain of retirement, when it comes, may be the greater. And can we do it, anyway? It may not be so easy, for example, for elder statesmen in the analytic world to go for clinical consultations with those they used to teach. To expose oneself in old age to the shock of the new and be excited by the creativity of younger generations means also dealing with our envy of those who are still productive and who will still be there to enjoy the excitement when we are not.

The consulting room that earlier one worked so hard to create is becoming, now, an emptier place. It is some time since the last patient came who was older than oneself. Age limits for taking students into analysis are a particular reminder for training analysts that the horizon is shortening and that powers are bound to fail. One may still be dependent on fees, however, for old age can bring its own financial problems. Throughout one's career, the consulting room has been the external representation of an internal analytic space. Now that less analysis is happening within it, does that mean there is less analytic functioning in that psychic space inside ourselves? Trust that the analytic identity we spent years establishing really did produce solid and enduring work will help us either to lay it aside well, or to go on being sustained by it.

Alongside such self-examination, ageing analysts also have to wonder how their colleagues see them. Is one still thought suitable to refer a patient to, who might need years of analysis? How well is one's physical health (above all, one's sense of hearing) holding up? There may be a temptation to take on whatever sort of work will reassure ourselves and our colleagues that we are still capable. The sense of being under judgement from one's peers comes round again, not formally now, but with an unspoken, unacknowledged scrutiny, to see how well we are still doing. And the hierarchy has reversed. This time it is the judgement, not of the training or student progress committees, nor of a membership or training analyst panel, but of our juniors that we are looking out for.

Analysts closing their careers are in a surprisingly similar position, we think, to newly qualified analysts beginning them. They are both at the end of an extraordinary process of development. This has brought them to a threshold where an identity that has become familiar must be left behind, or transformed into something unknown. In that unknown, there may be a great sense of potential, but it also arouses doubt, fear, and confusion. At the beginning and at the end of one's analytic life, all this has to be worked through in a condition of peculiar aloneness. Our seminar group for beginning analysts has been appreciated in the British Society. It seems much more difficult for psychoanalytic organizations to give thought to the corresponding issues for analysts ending their working lives, and they may do so only when problems arise which force them to. This resistance is not surprising. The capacity of all human beings to face old age and death depends on how they have been able to make use of the developmental processes of their lives, from infancy, through adolescence, into and throughout adulthood. The capacity of ageing analysts to face the dissolution of a working life depends likewise on how they have been able to use the processes and milestones of that life to develop and consolidate their analytic identities. Both for individual analysts and for analytic communities, it matters to view the analytic life cycle as an organic whole, no part of which exists in isolation from the rest.

Endnote

1. This paper is revised from one first presented at a Scientific Meeting of the British Psycho-Analytical Society on Wednesday 15 March, 2000. The authors are indebted to the discussion on that occasion, and to all their colleagues who have been members of the seminar described in the paper.

EPILOGUE

In the fearful years of the Yezhov terror I spent seventeen months in prison queues in Leningrad. One day somebody "identified" me. Beside me, in the queue, there was a woman with blue lips. She had, of course, never heard of me; but she suddenly came out of that trance so common to us all and whispered in my ear (everyone spoke in whispers there): "Can you describe this?" And I said: "Yes I can". And then something like the shadow of a smile crossed what had once been her face.

—Anna Akhmatova, 1 April 1957, Leningrad

Gathered together, the themes of this book express a strong leaning towards the development of states of freedom in analysis. This ranges from the need for the analysand to find new ways of expression both in relation to him- or herself and towards the other, as opposed to running along the old tramways laid down by personal histories caught up in and repeated by the transference dynamic, to the question of how best the analyst can develop his or her personal practice of psychoanalysis. A central part of this discussion, as I have argued, must involve an examination of the theory and practice of psychoanalytic training itself.

Yet the very theme of freedom and my associated word "tramways" leads my thoughts to the train lines which led from many countries to the death camps of Europe. European culture has never been free of aggression, stretching from medieval times through to the Enlightenment and culminating in the world wars fought on our soil in the twentieth century. This was Freud's legacy, but it is also undoubtedly our own and has played its part in the evolution of psychoanalysis throughout Europe. Freud, living through the First World War, attempted to make sense of the mass slaughter of nationals, despite or due to cultural heritage, and also had to flee Nazi Vienna, with his sisters not escaping and dying in concentration camps. What would it have meant for the future development of psychoanalysis if the Nazis had killed the Father? How can one think about trauma in the individual without thinking of it in generational terms, as well as in terms of the cultural heritage that formed the backdrop to the development of psychoanalysis from within the Austro-Hungarian Empire? One of my concerns throughout this book is the interface between personal and historical trauma, what we can grasp of the innermost life of the patient and of the world he or she lives in, and by which he or she is so profoundly affected.

2010 was the centenary year of the International Psychoanalytical Association (IPA). It had been established in 1910 during the second Psychoanalytic Congress in Nuremburg. Nearly sixty years after the inception of the IPA, the European Psychoanalytic Federation (EPF) was founded in Rome in 1969 with sixteen European Societies. The evolution of the EPF can teach us a great deal, not only about the past, but also about the future(s) of psychoanalysis. It began by establishing a *Bulletin* to further communication amongst its members and a credo "to initiate discussion and encourage controversy". It was clear then that the role of the two bodies would be very different. It would be for the IPA to guarantee the quality of training carried out under its auspices, while the EPF would provide a meeting place for local societies wishing to work together towards a common goal. Since then, the Federation has not administered the European community, nor is it a geographical subdivision of the International, rather it continues as a meeting place for communication, research, and teaching, and for the development of psychoanalysis within the many cultures of Europe. One question today, which became central to my role as Vice President from 2008 to 2011 must be how to preserve the integrity and difference of the EPF in the increasingly complex world of psychoanalysis whilst in addition working together with our colleagues from the other regions and the IPA. This priority is in addition to present-day concerns about the very survival of psychoanalysis in the current climate of quick fixes and business solutions.

In the third *EPF Bulletin* of 1973, Daniel Widlocher wrote, "differences between the societies make for interest, while the similarities due to the homogeneity of European culture make it possible to draw relevant comparisons". Since that time, with the fall of the Berlin Wall and the re-opening of Europe from west to east, things have become much more complex. Homogeneity no longer exists in this complexity. Without doubt, Europe has been the leading arena for the development of new analytic societies. The EPF has moved from its early days when its members could all meet in smallish, more intimate conferences (rather like the first fifteen or so IPA congresses which were all held in Europe prior to the Second World War) to today, with a recent annual conference in London in 2010 having over seven hundred participants. The successful development of our profession in terms of the increase in numbers of European colleagues in more Societies brings with it the many problems of size and the inevitable move away from intimacy.

Forms of organization and meeting in the EPF are part of something profound about negotiating difference. It is a way of breaking down a sense of a large monolithic organization into a more manageable and friendly resource whilst simultaneously enabling a realization that no single analytic training contains the truth of analysis. Learning the many ways of approaching the patient is a great antidote to the narcissism of small and large differences. Such regular meetings are an essential resource for the future development of analysis in a growing and complex region. What we have been establishing with these approaches is a new form—not just about learning more about the complexities of psychoanalysis—but one that allows us to begin to listen contrapuntally, the expression coined by Edward Said, as a way of creatively negotiating and discriminating what can often be profoundly divergent ways of understanding both theory and practice. The barrier to recognition, often by ignorance or by ignoring that which we do not imagine of the other, becomes something to be faced, confronted, and argued against within a facilitating environment. Profound cultural differences can also be noticed and thought about.

In recent years, the EPF has welcomed the Belgrade Society, Polish Society, German Psychoanalytical Association (DPG), Dutch

Psychoanalytical Group, and the British Psychoanalytical Association as IPA Component Societies. In addition, Study Groups attending the biannual Council of Presidents have been established in Romania, Croatia, South Africa, Portugal, Lithuania, and, in 2010, Lebanon, with two groups now in Moscow and Istanbul. This is a mixture of developing analysis in places where it did not exist, as well as evolving new societies with different theory and practice in places where analysis is already established. Furthermore, the work of the Psychoanalytic Institute for Eastern Europe (PIEE) has continued with great enthusiasm, with many colleagues in eastern parts of Europe without analytic centres becoming individual IPA members. The European region is fast growing to include, at present, the Middle East, Australia, and now the first African analytic group! It is clear that we are dealing with psychoanalysis in a multicultural, multiethnic, multilingual set of complexities that are growing well beyond the bounds of an Austro-Hungarian historical model from Freud's day. The quest is to find analytic environments that are similar and different to each other. For instance, it is absolutely appropriate that the beginnings of African psychoanalysis find their own depth understandings that encompass their own histories, family and tribal cultures, magical prescriptions, and the vast outpourings of severe repression and trauma visited on the land for far too long. The task is great and profoundly necessary, utilizing the tools of psychoanalysis for clinical work and helping a society see its deep psychological wounds and possibilities for healing.

The new connection to Africa allows us to add another form of recognition to an already complex mix of histories. Many of our own societies have also emerged, whether sooner or later, from often profound historical traumas that for many of us remain part of our own lifetime. Totalitarian regimes with deep controls embedded in social, political, and family life have played their part in the unconscious dynamics of twenty-first-century cultural life and many analytic societies still bear such scars. War within parts of Europe has only recently ended—for the time being. The European tradition has its history, its deadness, and the possibility of radical construction within an atmosphere of a capacity to criticize. To be able to tolerate the Other without allowing domination, at the same time as recognizing complexity, is our modern heritage. In psychoanalysis lies freedom, or at least the potential for freedom. Working together across the boundaries of Societies and countries is an eloquent and worthy model for such depth understandings. Given the traumas of European history and the often intolerant matrix of belief in psychoanalytic societies, this is also bound to touch upon questions of mourning and might also provide a space for its expression. If such difficult psychic processes, born of all our different but convergent histories of the twentieth and twenty-first centuries, cannot be reflected in analytic thought and practice within our analytic societies, then where else?

In June 2010, at one of the European Psychoanalytic Federation annual clinical meetings, I was involved in organizing a weekend seminar for recently qualified analysts in Warsaw. Twenty-eight colleagues from analytic societies all over Europe attended and presented clinical analytic material in small groups to a panel of training supervisors. The location was evocative. In the evenings, many of the group enjoyed being in the beautiful old town square, which had been completely rebuilt in the post-war reconstruction. To many, the deception of being in the heart of the city centre was unrealized as it looked so ancient and well kept. A quarter of the city had been the container for the Warsaw ghetto, which was totally razed during the 1943 Jewish uprising. The following year, most of the core central parts of the city were also razed during the Polish resistance partisans' uprising against the Nazi occupation before the Red Army advanced into Warsaw. Eighty-five per cent of the city was demolished. The destroyed city was lovingly recreated by copying Canaletto's famous views of the original city. We can read in this process a societal and cultural equivalent of how an individual's trauma is atomized and detached from the possibility of understanding such that it can only be viewed from the outside. Unknowing of its history, the visitor delights in the perfectly reconstructed environment. Yet what is this reconstruction, which hardly shows any link to its real past? Outside the castle, in the centre of the old town, is a small photo showing nothing of the vast destroyed building, other than its forlorn gateway and its right-hand corner showing a tottering thin pile of bricks. Knowing the destruction means that what one gazes upon holds within its view that which was wiped out. It exists in the negative shadow of what we see before us. This is part of the European city patch over the place where originally a rent had appeared. Freud, as already noted, puts it in relation to psychosis, "the delusion is found applied like a patch over the place where originally a rent had appeared in the ego's relation to the external world" (Freud 1924, p. 151). The city cannot bear to contemplate the tear in its own past and its population as well, unless courageous mental work is undertaken.

Such patches of architectural memory can be found all over Europe, the only partly recognized signs of a missing history in many important landscapes. It has not been easy to build the edifices that enable us to mourn our bloody European heritage and which provide an atmosphere to facilitate such mourning (Young 1993). Germany has had a long journey on this path: from the Mitscherlichs' important book, *The Inability to Mourn* of 1967, which analysed the failure of the German people and society to acknowledge the crimes committed in the name of National Socialism, to the Berlin of today. Alexander Mitscherlich's earlier book, *Doctors of Infamy: The Story of the Nazi Medical Crimes*, when first published in 1949, so inflamed much of society that large numbers of this edition were bought up by the German Medical Society in order to suppress it.

This in itself, of course, has its own evocative history. Looking at the Berlin monuments which exist to remind citizens of the totalitarian past, there are two which strike me as being of particular interest, although perhaps only one of them is truly significant or effective in this context. The first is the site at which the Nazis burnt the books, including Freud on psychoanalysis, on 10 May 1933. It now contains a monument consisting of a small glass window flat in the ground that looks deep into the underground, into an empty library with rows of bare shelves. Evocative certainly, yet as one walks away from the site, it becomes invisible from any distance. The ordinary passer-by is not even aware that it is there. The event is certainly remembered but only if one is standing right on top of the spot. The dictum out of sight, out of mind comes to my mind. The other monument in Berlin, which commemorates the Murdered Jews of Europe, consists of 2,700 concrete slabs near the Brandenburg Gate. This is a work that is not hidden away but daily in the sight of all who pass by in the very centre of the city. It points the way unequivocally to that which is known and needs to be seen. It is unavoidable and an essential part of the regeneration of national soul and spirit by the constant confrontation with destruction. The prose of Akhmatova at the start of this epilogue bears testament to daring to be able to describe that which is nearly too painful to bear being brought into the present in words. And yet it can be done.

We can relate this question of historical trauma and how it is registered in or refused by the mind to the analytic process. All crises, historical and personal, are at once endings and beginnings. In time, the existence of a crisis allows for the development of thoughts both of its origins as well as how it may end. There is always something unpredictable and potentially, even radically, unsettling about this. To take a metaphor, the apparently simple commencement of a Beethoven symphony can evoke an unconscious expectation, not just of its development, but how the composer will be able to dare to end what he has created. Great works often end in a dissonant way in relation to our milder, more humdrum expectations, exposing the listener to the shock of another, different resolution. Similarly, free association contains a potential for a radical edge that can move us away from the neat hedgerows of the narrative plot of known object relationships. Instead, it allows us to find ourselves in a dissonant landscape and not necessarily the one that we might have tried to creep towards. With understanding, free association can place us at such cardinal positions and we then have to try and understand where we are. These are different places from where we want to be, desire to be, or where society demands that we be. This is the reason why all totalitarian regimes in their control of society detest the possibility of thinking for oneself, separate from the group narrative.

Again, we can draw an analogy with the role of the analyst. Some analysands can act in a similar way to a dissonant in the ranks, breaking free from the dominant, known rhetoric of family life. Issues of dominance and passivity, as we have encountered in the clinical setting of these chapters, are a common facet of family life, spread around the various players. The analyst is unconsciously expected to play a double role, of quietly being part of that old regime whilst at the same time being in a separate mental place in order to notice and help create a disturbance from the fixity that has hitherto ruled the family and their individual mental states.

This process is never easy. It would be wrong to view the end of an analysis as offering a simple resolution as in "all's well that ends well". As Frank Kermode suggests in his famous essay *The Sense of an Ending*, "This is not, after all, quite the world of those who seek 'the courage to be and strip reality of the protection of myth'" (Kermode 2000). It is always a continuing struggle for the analysand to find that state of being which is distinct from immersion in one's primary narrative. Analysis can be an act of freedom against the chains of imposed and self-imposed narratives from family history and unconscious romance, but it also has to struggle against the passive expectation that something will be done by someone else, which often expresses itself as the desire for this to be the analyst's function. One of the issues to emerge strongly from these essays is how central these issues of freedom and emancipation are to the analytic process.

For me, the question that remains is how to foster the most painful forms of memory while keeping the spirit of free psychoanalytic enquiry alive. It was in the context of such concerns that in July 2005, Christopher Bollas and I formed "theothergroup" (TOG) in London. The group was an attempt to establish a new analytic forum with certain key values that were thought to be essential to analysis but which we felt were vulnerable, and often in danger of rupture. It encompassed a range of psychoanalytic viewpoints. The *"other"* in the group's name alluded to Freud's concept of the unconscious—which he termed *"ein anderer Schauplatz"* (Freud 1900, p. 48)—and to Ferenczi's emphasis on the actual other. The founding members of the group shared Freud's principle that the cornerstone of good analytic practice is for the analyst to listen to the analysand in a state of evenly suspended attentiveness which, if not, in Bion's terms, a state wholly without memory or desire, nonetheless strives to be free of prejudice. The group re-affirmed Freud's vision of the analysand's right to freedom of thought and speech in the presence of the psychoanalyst, commonly referred to as "free association". We thought that particular ways of enabling thinking together in a group, utilizing contrapuntal listening to include all ideas without imposing a narrowing of theory that can quickly develop into frank prejudice, would be valuable as an analytic listening tool.

There are clinical positions which have emerged over a long period of time within the changing context and historical evolution of the British Society, notably the legacy of the controversies in the 1950s over the work of Anna Freud and Melanie Klein and the ascendance in the Society of one theory of interpretation. Of course, we are aware that differing theories are different forms of perception, each deserving appropriate understanding and respect. Nonetheless, as we see it, some positions impede the spirit of analytical neutrality and interfere with free association, and in doing so block the process of access to a wider range of analytic ideas. What might be called an ethics of listening applies both to psychoanalytic work with analysands as well as to colleagues, as we listen to both the conscious and unconscious. To acknowledge the many differing concepts of mind and relationship in psychoanalysis is a further application of the ethics of listening. My own recent work has been in the context of the EPF where there are not just many types and theories of analytic training and clinical practice, but also many languages spoken and heard. I see it as a crucible where the above ideas might be developed into a new European analytic dialogue which, in its openness, would be truly in the spirit of Freud's legacy. The capacity to speak together ethically is the best way of preventing authoritarianism in our practice as well as in our European history. This is even more important today with the recent global financial crisis exposing the return of the repressed world of selfishness and the need to re-find an object to blame, be it the Taliban, Muslims, and always the ubiquitous Jew. As many European societies lurch more to the right, and human values seem to be polarized into a primitive dichotomy of "us and them", the spectre of totalitarianism returns to haunt us all. More than ever, an analytic thinking space is necessary as one form of resisting the lurch into domination both in society and in family life.

In his 2010 volume of poetry *Human Chain*, Seamus Heaney writes of the need to find an appropriate balance of contradictory positions: "The need on the one hand for a truth telling that will be hard and retributive, and on the other hand, the need not to harden the mind to a point where it denies its own yearnings for sweetness and trust." We are back in a contrapuntal world, of words that need to be spoken and longings that must be recognized, a world that might be thought again in terms of Ferenczi's "elasticity", holding the tensions, as they differ from time to time, both in analysis and within society.

There is also—appropriately for an epilogue—a question here about how to end. The end is ever present in our living out of life, for the individual and for society as well as in an analysis. The individual runs mythically from moment to moment, whilst our culture runs in grander aliquots from year to year, the century, or the pull of millennium. The IPA recognizes its century as if the survival of psychoanalysis is contingent on the magic of one hundred years (not incompatible with the idea that psychoanalysis as a discipline, a *mere* hundred years old, is still a child or adolescent). Kermode contrasts big centuries of time with the insistent ticking of the clock that pulls us along our journey from birth to death. The commencing movement in the sound "tick" he describes as a humble genesis to the more guttural sound of "tock", a type of feeble apocalypse, and the pause being the gap of life in between. The narrative structure is directed in a formulaic direction from then to now. Kermode then suggests that we might instead hear the sequence differently as tock-tick (Kermode 2000, p. 45). In this tiny metaphor, he breaks through to dissonance and invites us to view the well-ordered sequence as a potentially fractured noise. Of course, the life of an individual can be conceptualized in its forward-moving dynamic. Yet if we are to think about the structure of beginning and end and insert the tock first, the time interval, despite being the same, carries a very different resonance. It contains the dissonance, which is the stuff our patients bring us. The clock needs resetting, in its perceptions of the dominance of dissonant rhythms.

The tick-tock is a human narrative to fill the void of time as the clock moves ever forward. Psychoanalysis has a freedom to mentally escape such shackles and to go backwards in time when necessary, in order to re-find the lost objects or history of the patient. This is the value too of *après coup* or *Nachträglichkeit*, that allows the possibility of going back in time and unconsciously re-evaluating etchings on the mind. Re-finding lost objects is of course in itself another mythical quest, but one in which there can be a rebalancing of what can feel like the magical drive of destiny so that the individual may own more responsibility for his or her own causality. This means moving out of the groove of a slavish, unconscious drive to continue the life one has grown up with, including its perceptions and misperceptions, as if our character and object relationships have been fixed by the contingencies of life as something concrete that cannot, must not, be altered. Beneath the phantasy that things are fixed for all time resides the fear of and then what? What is to be made of life in the empty space without the patch that seems to hold it all together. Again, this is a place where psychoanalytic dialogue can be formative, allowing the concrete patch to be prised away so that a new healing can begin. To be able to have the freedom to have an adventure, to be alive in one's life, and to include being alive even as the long shadow descends into the dark.

REFERENCES

Abraham, K. (1921). Contribution to a discussion on tic. In: *Selected Papers on Psychoanalysis* (pp. 323–325. London: Karnac Books, 1997.

Abraham, N. & Torok, M. (1973). Self-to-self affliction: notes of a conversation on "psychosomatics". In: *The Shell and the Kernel: Renewals of Psychoanalysis, Volume 1.* Chicago: University of Chicago Press, 1994.

Aisenstein, M. (2010). Letter from Paris. *International Journal of Psycho-Analysis, 91*(3), June: 463–468.

Akhmatova, A. (1912). Alisa. In: R. Reeder (Ed.), *The Complete Poems* (p. 100). Saint Paul, MN: Zephyr Press.

Akhmatova, A. (1999). *In Scanning the Century* (Ed. P. Forbes). Harmondsworth: Penguin.

Appelfeld, A. (2005). Quoted in *The Observer Book Review,* 21 August.

Artaud, A. (1958). The Theatre and its Double. Grove Press p. 141.

Balint, A. & Balint, M. (1939). On transference and counter-transference. In: M. Balint, *Primary Love and Psycho-Analytic Technique.* London: Hogarth Press, 1952.

Balint, E. (1993). *Before I Was I—Psychoanalysis and the Imagination* (Ed. J. Mitchell & M. Parsons). London: Free Association.

Balint, M. (1935). Critical notes on the theory of the pregenital organizations of the libido. In: *Primary Love and Psycho-Analytic Technique.* London: Hogarth Press, 1952.

Balint, M. (1957). *The Doctor, His Patient and the Illness*. London: Pitman.

Balint, M. (1968). *The Basic Fault*. London: Tavistock.

Baranger, M., Baranger, W. & Mom, J. M. (1988). The infantile psychic trauma from us to Freud: pure trauma, retroactivity and reconstruction. *International Journal of Psycho-Analysis, 69*: 113–128.

Berlin, I. (2006). Two concepts of freedom. In: *Political Ideas in the Romantic Age*. London: Chatto and Windus.

Bion, W. R. (1961). *Experiences in Groups and Other Papers*. London: Tavistock.

Bion, W. R. (1962). Learning from experience. In: *Seven Servants*. New York, NY: Aronson, 1977.

Bion, W. R. (1970). Attention and interpretation. In: *Seven Servants*. New York, NY: Aronson, 1977.

Bollas, C. (1987). *The Shadow of the Object: Psychoanalysis of the Unthought Known*. London: Free Association.

Bollas, C. (1989). *Forces of Destiny—Psychoanalysis and Human Idiom*. London: Free Association.

Bollas, C. (1992). *Being a Character*. New York: Hill and Wang.

Bollas, C. (2000). *Hysteria*. London: Routledge.

Bollas, C. (2009a). *The Evocative Object World*. London: Routledge.

Bollas, C. (2009b). *The Infinite Question*. London: Routledge.

Breuer, J. & Freud, S. (1893–1895). *Studies on Hysteria. Standard Edition, Volume 2*.

Buechler, S. (1998). The analyst's experience of loneliness. *Contemporary Psychoanalysis, 34*: 91–113.

Casement, P. (1985). *On Learning from the Patient*. London: Tavistock.

Cooper, A. (1986). Some limitations on therapeutic effectiveness: the "burnout syndrome" in psychoanalysts. *Psychoanalysis Quarterly, 55*: 576–598.

Danckwardt, J. F. & Wegner, P. (2007). Performance as annihilation or integration? *International Journal of Psycho-Analysis, 88*: 1117–1133.

Dante (1984). *The Divine Comedy: Volume 1 The Inferno*. Harmondsworth: Penguin.

De Simone, G. (1997). *Ending Analysis: Theory and Technique*. London: Karnac Books.

Dewald, P. & Schwartz, H. (1993). The life cycle of the analyst: pregnancy, illness, and disability. *Journal of the American Psychoanalytic Association, 41*: 191–207.

Eissler, K. (1974). On some theoretical and technical problems regarding the payment of fees for psychoanalytic treatment. *International Review of Psycho-Analysis, 1*: 73–101.

Ellman, J. (1996). Analyst and patient at midlife. *Psychoanalysis Quarterly,* *65*: 353–371.

Etchegoyen, A. (1993). The analyst's pregnancy and its consequences on her work. *International Journal of Psycho-Analysis, 74*: 141–149.

Ferenczi, S. (1912). Transitory symptom-constructions during the analysis. In: *First Contributions to Psychoanalysis* (pp. 193–212). London: Hogarth, 1952.

Ferenczi, S. (1920). The further development of active therapy. In: *Further Contributions to the Theory and Technique of Psychoanalysis* (pp. 198–216). London: Hogarth, 1950.

Ferenczi, S. (1921). Psychoanalytical observations on tics. In: *Further Contributions to the Theory and Practice of Psychoanalysis* (pp. 142–173). London: Hogarth, 1950.

Ferenczi, S. (1925). Contra-indications to the "active" psychoanalytical technique. In: *Further Contributions to the Theory and Technique of Psychoanalysis* (pp. 217–229). London: Hogarth, 1950.

Ferenczi, S. (1928). The elasticity of psychoanalytic technique. In: *Final Contributions to the Problems and Methods of Psychoanalysis*. London: Hogarth, 1955.

Ferenczi, S. (1930). Fundamental traumatic effect of maternal hatred or of the lack of affection. In: *Final Contributions to the Problems and Methods of Psycho-Analysis* (p. 227). London: Hogarth, 1955.

Ferenczi, S. (1931a). Child-analysis in the analysis of adults. In: *Final Contributions to the Problems and Methods of Psycho-Analysis* (pp. 126–142). London: Hogarth, 1955.

Ferenczi, S. (1931b). Notes and fragments. In: *Final Contributions to the Problems and Methods of Psycho-Analysis* (p. 216). London: Hogarth, 1955.

Ferenczi, S. (1931c) On the revision of the *Interpretation of Dreams*. In: *Final Contributions to the Problems and Methods of Psychoanalysis*. London: Hogarth, 1955.

Ferenczi, S. (1932). *The Clinical Diary of Sandor Ferenczi* (Ed. J. Dupont). Cambridge, MA: Harvard University Press, 1988.

Ferenczi, S. (1933). Confusion of tongues between adults and the child. In: *Final Contributions to the Problems and Methods of Psychoanalysis* (pp. 156–167). London: Hogarth, 1955.

Ferenczi, S. & Freud, S. (1920–1933). *The Correspondence of Sigmund Freud and Sandor Ferenczi, Volume 3*. Cambridge, MA: Harvard University Press, 2000.

Ferraro, F. & Garella, A. (2009). *Endings: On Termination in Psychoanalysis*. New York: CPS Rodopi.

Fogel, G. & Glick, R. (1991). The analyst's postgraduate development—rereading Freud and working theory through. *Psychoanalysis Quarterly, 60*: 396–425.

Fortune, C. (Ed.) (2002). *Ferenczi–Groddeck Correspondence, 1921–1933*. London: Open Gate Press.

Foster, T. (1979). A cruise in a whale boat, and adventures in the Pacific Ocean. In: Melville, H. *Moby Dick or the Whale*. California: University of California Press.

Freud, A. (1963). The role of regression in mental development. In: *Research at the Hampstead Child Therapy Clinic and Other Papers, 1956–1965*. London: Hogarth, 1970, pp. 407–413.

Freud, S. (1900–1901). *The Interpretation of Dreams*, Parts 1 and 2. *Standard Edition, Volumes 4 and 5*.

Freud, S. (1905). *Three Essays on the Theory of Sexuality. Standard Edition, Volume 7*, pp. 123–246.

Freud, S. (1909). *Family Romances. Standard Edition, Volume 9*, pp. 235–242.

Freud, S. (1911). *Psycho-Analytic Notes on an Autobiographical Account of a Case of Paranoia (Dementia Paranoides). Standard Edition, Volume 12*, pp. 1–82.

Freud, S. (1911). *Formulations on the Two Principles of Mental Functioning. Standard Edition, Volume 12*, pp. 213–226.

Freud, S. (1914). *Remembering, Repeating and Working-Through (Further Recommendations on the Technique of Psycho-Analysis II). Standard Edition, Volume 12*, pp. 145–156.

Freud, S. (1915). *Words and Things*. Appendix C, *The Unconscious, Papers on Metapsychology. Standard Edition., Volume 14*, pp. 209–215.

Freud, S. (1918 [1914]). *From the History of an Infantile Neurosis. Standard Edition, Volume 17*, pp. 1–124.

Freud, S. (1919). *"A Child is Being Beaten": A Contribution to the Study of the Origin of Sexual Perversions. Standard Edition, Volume 17*, pp. 175–204.

Freud, S. (1920). *Beyond the Pleasure Principle. Standard Edition, Volume 18*, pp. 1–64.

Freud, S. (1924). *Neurosis and Psychosis. Standard Edition, Volume 19*, pp. 147–154.

Freud, S. (1925). *A Note Upon the "Mystic Writing-Pad". Standard Edition, Volume 19*, pp. 225–232.

Freud, S. (1928). *A Religious Experience. Standard Edition, Volume 21*, pp. 167–172.

Freud, S. (1937). *Analysis, Terminable and Interminable. Standard Edition, Volume 23*, pp. 209–254.

Freud, S. (1938). *An Outline of Psychoanalysis. Standard Edition, Volume 23*, pp. 139–208.

Freud, S. (1938). *Splitting of the Ego in the Process of Defence. Standard Edition, Volume 23*, pp. 271–278.

Gold, R. (1988). Transitional issues in the life cycle of the psychoanalyst (A Symposium). *Contemporary Psychoanalysis, 24*: 451.

Green, A. (1986). The dead mother. In: *On Private Madness* (pp. 142–173). London: Hogarth.

Gubrich-Simitis, I. (1984). From concretism to metaphor: thoughts on some theoretical and technical aspects of the psychoanalytic work with children of Holocaust survivors. *The Psychoanalytic Study of the Child, 39*: 301–319.

Heaney, S. (2010). *Human Chain*. London: Faber and Faber.

Imber, R. (1990). The avoidance of countertransference awareness in a pregnant analyst. *Contemporary Psychoanalysis, 26*: 223–236.

Jones, E. (1951). *Essays in Applied Psychoanalysis, Volume 2*. London: Hogarth.

Joseph, B. (1989). *Psychic Equilibrium and Psychic Change: The Selected Papers of Betty Joseph* (Ed. M. Feldman and E. Bott-Spillius). London and New York: Tavistock.

Kennedy, R. (1993). *Freedom to Relate*. London: Free Association.

Kermode, F. (2000). *The Sense of an Ending: Studies in the Theory of Fiction with a New Epilogue*. Oxford: Oxford University Press.

Khan, M. (1964). Ego Distortion, Cumulative Trauma and the Role of Reconstruction in the Analytic Situation, Int. J. Psychoanalysis, 45, pp. 272–278.

King, P. & Steiner, R. (Eds.) (1991). *The Freud–Klein Controversies 1941–1945*. London: Tavistock/Routledge.

Klauber, J. (1977). Analyses that cannot be terminated. In: *Difficulties in the Analytic Encounter* (pp. 63–76). New York: Aronson, 1981.

Klein, M. (1925). A contribution to the psychogenesis of tics. In: *Contributions to Psychoanalysis, 1921–1945*. London: Hogarth, 1948.

Klein, M. (1932). *The Psychoanalysis of Children*. London: Hogarth, 1973.

Kohon, G. (Ed.) (1986). *The British School of Psychoanalysis: The Independent Tradition*. London: Free Association.

Kohon, G. (1999). *No Lost Certainties To Be Recovered*. London: Karnac Books.

Laplanche, J. & Pontalis, J. B. (1973). *The Language of Psychoanalysis*. London: Hogarth and the Institute of Psycho-Analysis.

Layland, W. R. (1987). *A "Feasability" Study: The Ability to Set a Fee and Collect It*. Personal communication, unpublished paper.

Lear, J. (2000). *Happiness, Death and the Remainder of Life*. Cambridge, MA: Harvard University Press.

Lear, J. (2010). Review of *The Evocative Object World* and *The Infinite Question* by Christopher Bollas. *London Review of Books*, 11 March, pp. 34–35.

McDermott, V. A. (2003). Is free association still fundamental? *Journal of the American Psychoanalytic Association, 51*: 1349–1356.

Michaels, J. & Schoenberg, M. (1966). Some considerations of a retirement policy for training analysts. *Psychoanalytic Quarterly, 35*: 199–216.

Mitscherlich, A. & Mielke, F. (1949). *Doctors of Infamy: The Story of the Nazi Medical Crimes* (Trans. H. Norden). New York, NY: Schuman.

Mitscherlich, A. & Mitscherlich, M. (1967). *The Inability to Mourn: Principles of Collective Behavior*. New York: Random House, 1975.

Mollon, P. (2009). The foreclosure of the Freudian view of transference (as false connection) in modern technique. *The Bulletin of the British Psychoanalytic Society, 45*, 4 May: 26.

Parsons, M. (2000). *The Dove that Returns the Dove that Vanishes*. London and Philadelphia: Routledge.

Pontes, A. R. N. (2010). Sándor Ferenczi's *Clinical Diary* in our current psychoanalytic practice: Franco Borgogno, moderator. *International Journal of Psycho-Analysis, 91(5)*, October: 1224–1226.

Proust, M. (1921–1925). *Sodom and Gomorrah, The Prisoner*, and *The Fugitive*. In: *In Search of Lost Time* (Trans. John Sturrock). London: Allen Lane, 2002.

Quinodoz, J. (1996). The sense of solitude in the psychoanalytic encounter. *International Journal of Psycho-Analysis, 77*: 481–496.

Rayner, E. (Ed.) (1990). *The Independent Mind in British Psychoanalysis*. London: Free Association.

Rickman. J. (1950). On the criteria for the termination of an analysis. In: *Selected Contributions to Psychoanalysis*. London: Hogarth, 1957.

Rickman, J. (1957). Number and human sciences. In: *Selected Contributions to Psychoanalysis*. London: Hogarth, 1957.

Rilke, R. M. (1920). *Selected Poems*. Harmondsworth: Penguin, 1985.

Rosenbloom, S. (1992). The development of the work ego in the beginning analyst: thoughts on identity formation of the psychoanalyst. *International Journal of Psycho-Analysis, 73*: 117–126.

Rosenfeld, H. A. (1987). *Impasse and Interpretation*. London and New York: Tavistock.

Sandler. J. (1985). Towards a Reconsideration of Psychoanalytic Theory of Motivation. *Bul. Anna Freud. 8*: 223–244.

Shakespeare, W. (1605). *King Lear*. Harmondsworth: Penguin Books, 2007.

Shane, M. (1977). A rationale for teaching analytic technique based on a developmental orientation and approach. *International Journal of Psycho-Analysis, 58*: 95–108.

Sklar, J. (2010). *Manifesto for EPF Presidency*. Unpublished paper.

Smith, H. (2001). Hearing voices: the fate of the analyst's identifications. *Journal of the American Psychoanalytic Association, 49*: 781–812.

Strachey, J. (1934). The nature of the therapeutic action of psycho-analysis. *International Journal of Psycho-Analysis, 15*: 127–159.

Szalita, A. (1985). On becoming a psychoanalyst: education or experience. *Contemporary Psychoanalysis, 21*: 130–142.

Szecsödy, I. (2001). Letter to John Steiner. *International Journal of Psycho-Analysis, 82*: 171–173.

Taylor, G. J. (1993). Clinical application of a dysregulation model of illness and disease: a case of spasmodic torticollis. *International Journal of Psycho-Analysis, 74*: 581–595.

Tolstoy, L. (1877). *Anna Karenina*. London: Everyman, 1992.

Wallerstein, R. S. (1981). *Becoming a Psychoanalyst: A Study in Psychoanalytic Supervision*. New York: International Universities Press.

Widlocher, D. (1973). *Psychoanalysis in Europe Bulletin, 3*: 1–5.

Winnicott, D. W. (1957). Hallucinations and dehallucinations. In: *Psychoanalytic Explorations*. Cambridge, MA: Harvard University Press, 1992.

Winnicott, D. W. (1958). The capacity to be alone. *International Journal of Psycho-Analysis, 39*: 416–420.

Winnicott, D. W. (1960a). The theory of the parent–infant relationship. In: *The Maturational Processes and the Facilitating Environment: Studies in the Theory of Emotional Development*. London: Hogarth, 1965.

Winnicott, D. W. (1960b). Ego distortion in terms of true and false self. In: *The Maturational Processes and the Facilitating Environment: Studies in the Theory of Emotional Development*. London: Hogarth, 1965.

Winnicott, D. W. (1971). The use of an object. In: *Playing and Reality*. Harmondsworth: Penguin.

Winnicott, D. W. (1988). *Human Nature*. London: Free Association.

Yerushalmi, Y. H. (1982). *Zakhor—Jewish History and Jewish Memory*. Seattle and London: University of Washington Press.

Young, J. E. (1993). *The Texture of Memory—Holocaust Memorials and Meaning*. New Haven: Yale University Press.

INDEX